# People of the Mesa Verde Country

## *An Archaeological Remembrance*

---

## by Ian M. Thompson

Illustrations by Richard Cornelius

Foreword by Russell Martin

Afterword by Jonathan Thompson

EarthTales Press

WESTCLIFFE PUBLISHERS

www.westcliffepublishers.com

**International Standard Book Number:** 1-56579-474-5

© Crow Canyon Archaeological Center, 2002. All rights reserved.

Crow Canyon Archaeological Center
23390 County Road K
Cortez, CO 81321
www.crowcanyon.org

**Editors:**   Manuscript Editor, Jane Kepp
Content Editor, Jake Adam York
Copy Editor, Peg Tremper
Managing Editor, Jenna Samelson Browning

**Designer:** Angie Lee, Grindstone Graphics, Inc.
**Production Manager:** Craig Keyzer

**Published by:**
Westcliffe Publishers, Inc.
EarthTales Press
P.O. Box 1261
Englewood, CO 80150
www.westcliffepublishers.com

**Printed by:** Transcontinental Printing, Canada

**Library of Congress Cataloging-in-Publication Data:**
Thompson, Ian, 1940-1998.
  People of the Mesa Verde country : an archaeological remembrance / by
Ian M. Thompson ; illustrations by Richard Cornelius ; foreword by
Russell Martin ; afterword by Jonathan Thompson.
      p. cm.
Includes bibliographical references.
  ISBN 1-56579-474-5
  1. Indians of North America--Four Corners Region--Antiquities. 2.
Archaeologists--Four Corners Region--History. 3. Excavations
(Archaeology)--Four Corners Region--History. 4. Four Corners
Region--Antiquities.  I. Title.
  E78.S7 T488 2002
  979.2'5901--dc21
                                2002016169

*For more information about other fine books and calendars from Westcliffe Publishers, please contact your local bookstore, call us at 1-800-523-3692, write for our free color catalog, or visit us on the Web at* **www.westcliffepublishers.com.**

**An aerial view of the Mesa Verde area.** © Walter BigBee, *Comanche*, 2001.

# Acknowledgments

✳

The production of this book has been a lengthy process that involved a number of people, and we gratefully acknowledge their collective efforts. Ricky Lightfoot, Russell Martin, Gayle Prior, Ruth Slickman, Jonathan Thompson, and Mark Varien collaborated and designed the initial template for the book. Ruth and Jonathan were particularly helpful in compiling and organizing Sandy's unfinished manuscript and his previous writings. Jane Kepp compiled and edited the first draft and David Grant Noble read and commented on it. Bill Lipe, Mark Varien, Ruth Slickman, and Jonathan Thompson worked with this initial draft to develop the manuscript that was submitted for publication.

Many of Sandy's friends knew that he was very excited about the prospect of working with Crow Canyon archaeologists to write a book about the archaeology of the Four Corners region which he loved so passionately. When word spread that Sandy had been diagnosed with terminal cancer, his friends came to him wanting to know how they could help. His response was that they could contribute to a publication fund at Crow Canyon that would support books on Southwestern archaeology written for the general public. His friends responded by contributing to the Ian Thompson Celebration Fund at Crow Canyon, and the publication of this book was supported in part by that fund. Sandy would have wanted to recognize each person who contributed to it, and the Crow Canyon staff would like to thank the following: Betsy and Cliff Alexander, Charmay Allred, Edward Angus, Anonymous, Leon Bailey, Julian Baker, Ballantine Family Fund, Mary Lyn and Richard Ballantine, William Ballantine, Mary Beaston, Anne Beckett, Harold Bendigkeit, Tonia Bennett, Sandra and Herbert Billings, Margaret and Roland Bixler, Dennis Boon, Marcia Boon, Pete Boyce, Gene Bradley, Barbara and David Breternitz, Eileen and John Brown, Lynn and Norman Brown, Robert and John Bryant, Ann Butler, Joyce and Bruce Chelberg, Robert Colgan, Roy Craig, Barbara and Nance Creager, Marjorie Crosby, Edward Crump, Mr. and Mrs. Myron Darmour, S. Davie and the Garden Mercantile, Jane Dillard, Raymond Duncan, Donald Edvalson, Pat and Stanton Englehart, Francis English, Elizabeth Feazel, George Feldman, Jeanne and Charles Fischer, Wendy Fisher, Gerald Franchini, Charlotte and David Gibson, Angelina and A.L. Gladson, Nancy and Owen Godwin, Joan Goldstein, Melissa Gould and Ricky Lightfoot, Robert Greenlee, Joyce and Bruce Grimes, Marilyn and Charles Haley, Martha and James Hartman, Shelley and

Robert Hatfield, Karen and Alden Hayes, Michelle Hegmon, William Hensler, Robert Heyder, John Hopkins, Sally and Charles Hubbard, Indian Camp Ranch, C. Paul Johnson, J. M. Jones, Karol and James Kleidon, Ida Sink Kolb, Alex and Skip Lange, La Plata Archaeological Consultants, Aleta Lawrence, Stephen Lekson, Linda Martin, Clara and Roy Mason, Charles McAfee, Neil McCallum, Alice McClain and Lynn Waltz, Robert A. McClevey, Jr., James Mead, Andrea Messer, Sarah Monk, Wayne Moorhead, John Nelson, Leah and Perry Pahlmeyer, Stuart Patterson, Dottie Peacock, Maxine and Carroll Peterson, Jean and Charles Peterson, Virginia Pool and Richard Wilshusen, Michael Preston, Margaret Ptolmy, Anne and Norman Putnam, Nancy Clark Reynolds, Dorothy and Rex Rice, Fran and Burt Rissman, Sue Anschutz-Rodgers, Dylan Schwindt, Michael Shafer, Lila and James Sholes, Barbara Shore, Daniel Slickman, Ruth Slickman, Duane Smith, Stuart Struever, L. G. Sullivan, Sidney Taylor, Marianne Teetsel, Marilyn Thompson, Jennifer and Robert Usher, Shaila Van Sickle and John Sanders, Carla Van West, Mark Varien, Merrill and Richard Varien, Eileen Veach, Gomer Walters, Edward Wasson, Mary and James Welch, Ann Willard, Judy and Gordon Wilson, Stanley Yake, Gerald Zink, Patti and Ed Zink, and Ruby Zink.

Cassandra Leoncini directed the final production of the manuscript, coordinating the efforts of many. Jake Adam York edited the final manuscript, and Richard Cornelius created the original pen-and-ink illustrations and the cover art. Cassandra Leoncini, Shirley Dennison, Robert McDaniel, Sandy Tradlener, and Kristen Kuckelman compiled the photographs for the book. Frank Lister and Mark Stroud produced the map of the Four Corners region especially for this work. Tom Auer helped with the final manuscript preparation. We gratefully acknowledge the enthusiasm of John Fielder and Linda Doyle at Westcliffe Publishers.

Finally, Sandy would have wanted to acknowledge those who worked with him to develop the contents of this book: Andrew Fowler, Ricky Lightfoot, William Lipe, Tessie Naranjo, John Stein, Rina Swentzell, Mark Varien, and Richard Wilshusen. To the many other supporters and friends who offered their assistance to Sandy and to Crow Canyon in this project, we extend our deepest appreciation.

# Contents

✳

**Opposite: An ancient Puebloan tower in McElmo Canyon, photographed at the turn of the 19th century.** Photo courtesy of Colorado Historical Society (10028082).

# Foreword

✳

Ian ("Sandy") Thompson lived virtually all his life in a single place. Except for infant years in southern California and Chicago, and parts of his early adulthood in Boulder, Colorado, he spent the rest of his too-few days in the Four Corners country, a place that came to belong to him over the course of the five decades he spent exploring and writing about its gloriously diverse collection of mountains, deserts, and plains. The region where Arizona, Colorado, New Mexico, and Utah meet has been home to humans for 12,000 years, and Ian Thompson was always captivated by the ways in which people lived—often successfully, sometimes calamitously—in a landscape that is at once challenging and inspiriting, difficult and curiously divine. He wrote extensively over the years about the shape and texture of the land, about its moods and manners and seasons, but at the close of his life he cared foremost about the legacy of the Puebloan culture in the Four Corners country—how the culture had thrived in the first millennium of the Common Era, how it declined, and what those 1,000 years of habitation truly mean to those of us whose tenure here is only a fraction as long. When he died on April 20, 1998, at his home on the rim of Hartman Canyon in Cortez, Colorado, Sandy left behind a writing project intended to synthesize for general readers the archaeological research done in the region during the last quarter of the twentieth century and explain the arcane processes through which transcendent insight can sometimes be achieved by simple digging in the dirt.

The book you are holding is not the book he hoped to complete before his death, but a version of what he imagined and creatively set into motion a year before. This book, edited and published posthumously, is a grateful memorial to Ian Thompson, but more important, it is an opportunity for us to read the words of a man who understood, better than any other I have known, why the past matters as profoundly as it does.

During his 57 years, Sandy worked as a hard-rock miner, a dairy farmer, and a type-setter for the weekly newspaper he also edited. A bit reluctantly, he made a foray into politics in 1980, first with his election to the Durango, Colorado, city council, followed

**Ian "Sandy" Thompson, 1981.** © Dick Arentz, 1981.

by a two-year term as the city's mayor. In subsequent years, he became greatly sought after as a member of public and private boards, commissions, and committees—in large part because he possessed the rare ability to listen and because, temperamentally, he was more inclined to set projects into motion than to debate whether motion made sense. In 1970, Sandy joined the staff of *The Durango Herald* and served as associate editor for four years. From 1985 until six weeks before his death, he wrote a Sunday column for

the *Herald*, "Four Corners Almanac," a meditation on the land, history, and people of the region he observed so intimately and so well. A collection of those essays, *Houses on Country Roads*, was published in 1995 and was a finalist for the Colorado Book Awards.

When he moved to rural Montezuma County, Colorado, in 1984, Sandy had presumed that writing would occupy all of his time. But his passion for Puebloan archaeology—combined with an utter inability to say "No" to people in dire need of his talents and expertise—led him to accept a position as executive director of the Crow Canyon Archaeological Center in Cortez in 1985. It was during his tenure at Crow Canyon's helm that the Center burgeoned into an internationally renowned, award-winning research and educational institution. In a reprise of

**"Sandy" Thompson at about age 12 in Peñasco, New Mexico.** Photo courtesy of Gerald Zink.

what he accomplished at the *Herald*, this essentially very private man again proved almost magically adept at managing and motivating those whose work he oversaw. Along the way, Sandy's staff grew fiercely dedicated to his vision of what Crow Canyon could become, and together they worked tirelessly to bring that vision to fulfillment. Although he took a break from the demands of the job in 1991, he was persuaded to return to Crow Canyon in 1995 as director of research. In 1997, he was named to the endowed Crow Canyon Chair, a position that allowed him to begin writing this book.

He looked forward to the opportunity to summarize the research that had taken place at Crow Canyon over the preceding decade by profiling many of the sun-seared men and women who conducted field research in remote pockets of the region. He wanted to compare—and occasionally sharply contrast—the perspectives and postulations of these talented young archaeologists with those of eloquent contemporary Puebloans whose ancestors were the subjects of this sharply focused anthropological investigation. Most of all, he wanted to explore his own evolving notion of community—the ways in which landscape determines the shape of lives lived in a particular place, how people go about the business of linking their lives together, how the land is a dear neighbor you never entirely get to know. He had just begun to dig deeply into this complex and promising new project when he learned that he was gravely ill, and that little time in the Four Corners country remained to him.

In measured response to that unwelcome news, Sandy chose not simply to revel in his final days, not solely to throw a pack on his back and head out to "look at sites" in the manner that always gave him such great delight, and certainly not to make his way to a warm seashore where he might contemplate a different part of the planet until his days were done. Instead, he and his physicians did what they could in the hope that he might stretch months of remaining life into a year or more. Then he set to work with an energy and focused determination that were unusual, even for him. He repeatedly visited the places and people that mattered most. He took time to speak and write frankly and eloquently about what it meant to have your days draw to a close too soon. The clear-eyed, inquisitive, and accepting way in which he faced what the universe had in store became a bounteous lesson for those of us he left behind.

His final manuscript was not yet complete in the spring of 1998 when his sons and friends sprinkled his ashes into the waters of Crow Canyon Creek and sent him off on a new and uncertain project. The book that he hadn't been able to finish had come very much to life before his death. Those same family members and friends set its eventual publication into motion because they knew it would wonderfully honor his memory, and because it made simple sense that his final words—like the hundreds of thousands that preceded them—would also find grateful readers. With editor Jane Kepp's assistance, Ricky Lightfoot, Ruth Slickman, Mark Varien, and Jonathan Thompson shepherded those words from typescript to print. His son Jonathan—now a fine writer as well—contributed a remarkable concluding essay that allows those who knew Sandy to hear his soft but resolute voice again and once more see the spring in his step as he walked out into the sage and juniper and sandstone that were his home.

What follows is some of the best of Ian Thompson's writing, words focused not on the homeland itself but rather on the people who chose the Four Corners country as the place where they would make their lives—ancient Puebloans, early homesteaders, and contemporary archaeologists alike. His perspective, as always, is essentially optimistic, certain as he is that discovering how to live successfully in a given landscape is a challenge that's asked of each of us, one at which we can succeed if we care to. Sandy Thompson wrote in a note to me a couple of years before his death, "I seem more and more to be working with people my sons' ages. They frequently refer to me as 'Mr. Thompson'. I no longer correct them. I go away from work sessions with these kiddos with more energy than I take to them. Which means I'm beginning to believe there is a future."

He was kidding me, of course. His life, his work, his finely crafted words prove absolutely that he had believed in the future for a very long time already, as fiercely as he did—and I suspect still does—believe in the past.

—**Russell Martin**
Salt Lake City, Utah
1999

**The north escarpment of Mesa Verde rising above the Montezuma Valley.** © Walter BigBee, *Comanche*, 2001.

# Preface

The Crow Canyon Archaeological Center, founded in 1983, is a nonprofit organization whose mission is to conduct archaeological research and public education programs in partnership with Native Americans and institutions with common interests. Sandy Thompson was involved with the Center from its inception, serving as chairman of its founding advisory committee (1982–1985), executive director (1985–1991), a member of its Board of Trustees (1985–1991), and director of research (1995–1997). Sandy was a visionary leader and, for many, the embodiment of the institution and what it sought to accomplish.

In 1997, Sandy resigned as the director of research and was named the Crow Canyon Chair, an endowed position that allowed him to devote himself to his two great passions: archaeology and writing. He could barely contain his excitement as he started on a book that he had seemingly been preparing to write for his entire life. Shortly after he began the project, he was diagnosed with terminal cancer. Rather than slowing him down, his illness intensified his passion to complete the book that he saw as his major lifework, and he worked furiously on it during a year when he also fought for his life. Sadly, he lost that fight April 20, 1998.

Sandy was not able to complete the book he had intended to write, but he left behind a partial manuscript and a large body of other written work. Crow Canyon took on the task of producing a book that combined the unfinished manuscript and selected pieces of Sandy's previous writings. That process involved many of his friends, colleagues, and supporters over a period of three years. It is with great pride and a sense of accomplishment that Crow Canyon can now share Sandy's final work with others who appreciate the beauty and the history of the Mesa Verde country.

**The Crow Canyon Archaeological Center.** © Walter BigBee, *Comanche*, 2001.

＊

## Chapter one

# *Ackmen, Land of Opportunity*

*Homesteaders who come here are seldom disappointed…. Dry farming is not an experiment—it is a success. The rainfall is about twenty inches and in nearly all cases falls at times of year it is most needed…. To the south and east lies the great Montezuma Valley which furnishes the drylander his hay…. Never before, young man, and men with families, has the west extended you a more cordial hand of welcome, never before has it offered you better opportunities to get a home. Especially do the home-loving people of Dolores and Montezuma counties' dry lands extend to you a glad hand and welcome you as a neighbor.*

—*Ackmen Pioneer Chieftain*
September 20, 1920

# June 24, 1997

I left my home in Cortez, Colorado, before sunrise and traveled northwest on Highway 666 up the long, gentle slope from the Montezuma Valley and onto the Great Sage Plain. A string of mountain peaks rising to more than 14,000 feet stood silhouetted against the brightening eastern sky. The highway skirted the heads of Alkali, Trail, and Yellow Jacket canyons, cutting toward the San Juan River beyond McElmo Dome. My route took me through the far-flung farms of the rural Arriola, Lewis, and Yellow Jacket communities before I turned off the asphalt onto a winding country road that led through a piñon and juniper forest.

Emerging from the forest into a gently rolling landscape of vast dryland fields of winter wheat and pinto beans, I pulled my pickup to a stop overlooking the head of Sandstone Canyon and the town site of Ackmen and stepped out into the first rays of the rising sun. Birdsong drifted down from the forest, and the sad songs of mourning doves floated up from the canyon rims. I looked down to where Ackmen, the Town of the Drylands, once stood. Nothing remains but a few foundations of the homes and businesses that once flourished there, now obscured by head-high sage.

The day warmed and the birds fell silent. I became aware of the sound of traffic speeding along the distant highway. That faint, endless sound hung over the head of Sandstone Canyon and the ghost of Ackmen. It was the sound that had spelled the end of the Town of the Drylands.

Visible in the fields stretching away in every direction from Sandstone Canyon were ancient rubble mounds, the remains of the houses of Pueblo Indian farm families who lived here until the end of the thirteenth century. In retrospect, the stories of those communities, to the degree they are known—each with its own beginning, middle, and end—would have had a familiar ring to the families who lived in twentieth-century Ackmen until its hard-fought demise in 1938.

When the archaeologist Paul S. Martin arrived there in 1928, Ackmen was a thriving rural center serving a community of scores of families who were clearing the wilderness

**Dryland farmer and son at work in their field, ca. 1915.** Photo courtesy of La Plata County Historical Society.

from their new homesteads. Unirrigated dryland farms spread out from that community hub for miles around.

In describing the area, Martin observed:

> Climatic conditions within this area have probably remained nearly the same for the past two or three thousand years. The Indians of yesterday probably had the same factors of environment against which to struggle as do the ranchers of today. Rainfall is scanty as a rule, although some seasons may be abnormally wet, as was that of 1929, while others may be unusually dry. Droughts are the rule, however. Springs are extremely scarce at present, although there is some evidence for believing that water in favorable seasons could be obtained in limited quantities by digging shallow wells in the canyon bottoms. The soil of the region is good, and when cleared of the omnipresent, useless sagebrush, will yield a fair crop if properly ploughed and tended. It is an uphill struggle, however, for the modern farmer, and it must have been equally hard, if not more difficult, for the prehistoric farmer.... Irrigation, in the sense of introducing water into cultivated areas by means of ditches, was unknown in ancient times, and even today no irrigation is possible in the area west and north of Ackmen.[1]

The town, though barely a dozen years old when Martin arrived, boasted a store and filling station, a garage, a school, bean-cleaning and storage facilities, a sawmill, a post office, a telephone company, a hotel, and numerous homes. Ackmen sat at the junction of two important early transportation routes: Old Bluff Road, which led from Cortez, Colorado, to Bluff, Utah, on the San Juan; and the Mormon Trail, which skirted the canyon heads between Cortez and Monticello, Utah, at the foot of the Abajo Mountains. For weary travelers on those routes, the Ackmen Hotel was a welcome overnight stop.

But the site of Ackmen was an important stop for travelers long before the routes were known by their present names and before the town was ever imagined. It lay by a spring in Sandstone Canyon, a stopping place for Spaniards following the Spanish Trail between Santa Fe, New Mexico, and the missions along the California coast. The first official Spanish explorers, in 1765 and 1776, were led along the trail by Indian guides who themselves followed a route that had surely been used by their predecessors since time immemorial.

Just below Ackmen, Sandstone Canyon, like several other canyons gashed into the Great Sage Plain, deepens dramatically until, in just a few miles, it is nearly 1,000 feet deep where it cuts through McElmo Dome at Sandstone's junction with Yellow Jacket Canyon. The canyons pose formidable barriers to anyone traversing the Great Sage Plain, and so the ancient route skirted the canyonheads on the eastern edges of the plain. Highway 666 follows the same route today for the same reason.

The canyonheads are frequently the sites of springs—important water sources for travelers on foot and horseback in an arid land. It was because turn-of-the-century travelers to Bluff and Monticello often camped at the spring in the head of Sandstone Canyon that James and Lura Hadley decided to establish a store and post office there in 1916. The hotel soon followed, and its beds must have been a welcome alternative to sleeping on the hard, bare slickrock of the canyon rims. Homesteaders flocked to the surrounding countryside in the early 1920s, and the town grew to serve their needs as well.

The school, founded in 1917, became the community's educational and social center. Homesteaders' children attended grade school and high school there, and whole families came from miles around to attend church services, dances, and potluck dinners. The

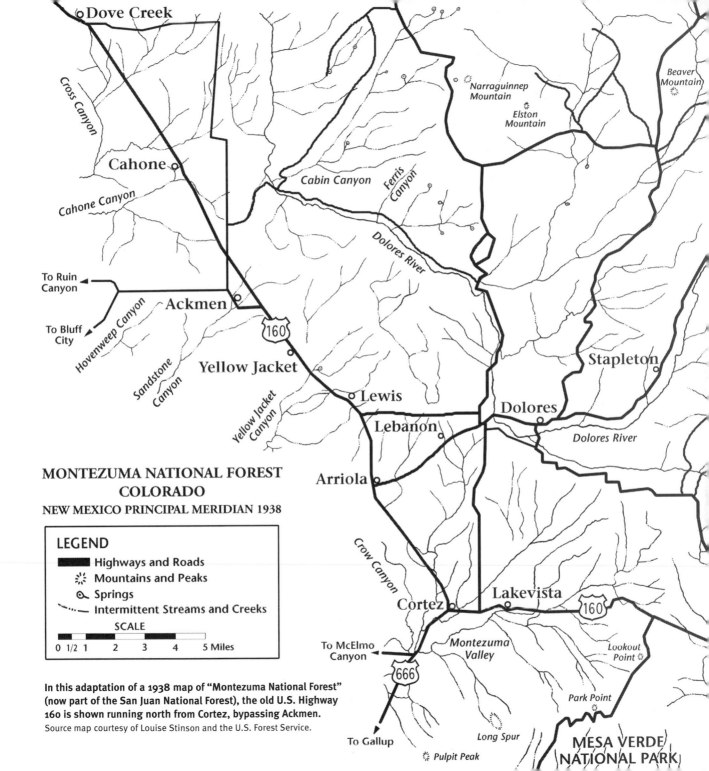

MONTEZUMA NATIONAL FOREST
COLORADO
NEW MEXICO PRINCIPAL MERIDIAN 1938

LEGEND

- ▬▬ Highways and Roads
- ☼ Mountains and Peaks
- ☙ Springs
- ‒‒‒ Intermittent Streams and Creeks

SCALE

0  1/2  1    2    3    4    5 Miles

In this adaptation of a 1938 map of "Montezuma National Forest"
(now part of the San Juan National Forest), the old U.S. Highway
160 is shown running north from Cortez, bypassing Ackmen.
Source map courtesy of Louise Stinson and the U.S. Forest Service.

**The excavation of two superimposed kivas at Lowry Ruin, not far from the Ackmen town site, ca. 1930.**

Photo courtesy of Colorado Historical Society (10028077).

members of the community knew they were a community simply because they knew where their children went to school and where they themselves went to pray, to dance, and to share food with their neighbors. The schoolhouse was owned, built, maintained, and used by the community as a whole, and it brought people together on a regular basis—a requirement of maintaining a sense of community. Geographical boundaries were defined by the outermost homesteads in the area.

The post office, general store, and school—places where people regularly came face to face—helped to maintain a sense of community. They are gone now. The schoolhouse no longer stands on the spot where it was built, but the community and its geographical boundaries still exist today. Only the center has moved.

In 1936, work began on a new highway between Monticello and Cortez linking the rural communities in between. Earlier foot and horse trails and the first vehicular roads followed the contours of the land because travelers preferred to wind back and forth around the canyonheads rather than expend energy going up and down across them. But modern road-building equipment and more powerful vehicles enabled the new highway to shoot

*A map of the San Juan River Basin looks like a rumpled bearskin rug thrown across the Four Corners where Arizona, Colorado, Utah, and New Mexico meet. The rug's tail is shoved up against the Continental Divide in the east, marking the headwaters of the San Juan River near Wolf Creek Pass in Colorado. The nose points west to where the basin narrows and the river joins the Colorado River in Lake Powell near Navajo Mountain in Utah. The rear leg in the north is formed by the drainage of the Animas River, which flows past the 14,000-foot Needle Mountains on its way toward Aztec Ruins National Monument and Farmington, New Mexico, where it flows into the San Juan. The front leg in the north is the Montezuma Creek drainage, which begins high in the Abajo Mountains. Montezuma Creek enters the San Juan in the modern Navajo community of that name in Utah. The rear southern leg of the rug is the drainage of the Chaco River, flowing northwest from the Continental Divide near Chaco Culture National Historical Park. The front leg on the south is the drainage of Chinle Creek, which begins high up in the Chuska Mountains just above Canyon de Chelly National Monument, Arizona. Chinle Creek enters the San Juan River where Comb Ridge crosses it just downstream from the historic Mormon farming community of Bluff, Utah.*

—Ian Thompson, 1997

nearly straight as an arrow, zigzagging slightly from rural center to rural center, between the two towns. Much of the labor on the new highway, now Highway 666, was done by men of the Civilian Conservation Corps (CCC). A large CCC camp went up on the outskirts of Ackmen, and its residents became a welcome addition to local social life. The young men sponsored community rodeos and races and crowded into schoolhouse dances to woo the belles of Ackmen.

This temporary excitement soon passed, and in the end Ackmen paid the ultimate price. The new highway missed it by a country mile. As the Great Depression eased, the pace of life quickened. Travelers no longer willingly detoured a mile to stay in the Ackmen Hotel. Why should they, when the 60-mile trip between Cortez and Monticello now took a couple of hours, instead of a couple of days? Calvin Denton, Ackmen's leading citizen, was the first to move. He took his bean mill and storage elevator 2 miles north to a location on the new highway and opened a general store there, too. Other businesses, the post office, and most families living in Ackmen soon followed and established New Ackmen.

The school, however—the real and symbolic center of the larger Ackmen community —stayed put. Ackmen diehards were determined that the schoolhouse would stay exactly where it was. By 1938, 23 students lived in New Ackmen, and three lived in Ackmen proper. School district residents voted overwhelmingly to move the school, building and all, to New Ackmen. Families split down the middle, brother against brother and mother against daughter, in the ensuing conflict. Ackmen's remaining residents took matters into their own hands, and in a face-to-face confrontation, stopped the "hijacking" of their beloved schoolhouse. They then charged voter fraud. After a second vote approved the move with an even greater majority, the residents of New Ackmen went into rapid action, and moved the school to its new location by the next morning.

To add insult to injury, they changed the name of New Ackmen to Pleasant View. Within a very short time, the frugal residents of the new town lifted every sound structure in Ackmen from their foundations and moved them to Pleasant View. Happily, the move was a short one, or families could not have taken their major possessions—from houses to farming equipment—with them. They left behind the town dump, an accumulation of

**Archaeologist Paul S. Martin at a site near Ackmen, ca. 1930.** Photo courtesy of Colorado Historical Society (10028075).

broken dishes, rusting tin cans, soda bottles, and ashes, unceremoniously dumped over the canyon rim.

Ackmen apparently vanished. But sometimes, the more things change, the more they stay the same. Only the community hub had moved, though not far, and its name had changed. The families on the widely dispersed homesteads around Pleasant View were the same families who had been there for years. The names on the mailboxes along country roads today are the same ones that were there in the late 1930s. The original rural community and its original geographical boundaries survived. The cemetery, hallowed ground where Ackmen's pioneers lie buried, continues in use today and may be the community's strongest surviving symbol. The grandsons and granddaughters of the pioneers, even those who have scattered to the far edges of the continent, make pilgrimages there now on Memorial Day, and the sense of community is renewed.

The history of Ackmen parallels, to one degree or another, those of at least a dozen other twentieth-century farming communities on the Great Sage Plain. And they parallel the histories of the more numerous ancient Puebloan farming communities that persisted and flourished on the plain for hundreds of years before the end of the thirteenth century.

**Archaeologist Dr. Paul S. Martin, ca. 1930.** Photo courtesy of Colorado Historical Society (10028083).

When Paul Martin first came to Ackmen in 1928, he had little interest in new Anglo–American communities. It was the stories of the ancient Indian communities he came to piece together from the silent remains of their houses and villages. In doing so, he unwittingly immortalized Ackmen in the annals of Southwestern archaeology when he named an important period in local Pueblo Indian history the "Ackmen–Lowry Phase." He inventoried hundreds of sites, and excavated several in the area, including Lowry Ruin. His work continued from 1928 to 1938, coincidentally Ackmen's final year of existence. Martin's decade of archaeological research on the Great Sage Plain marked the last major field project there until the Crow Canyon Archaeological Center began a much more ambitious program of field research. Beginning with the ruins of an ancient hamlet called Duckfoot and a larger site called Sand Canyon Pueblo, both south of Ackmen, Crow Canyon's research continues today. It is designed to build a detailed picture of the histories of the ancient people, households, and communities of the Great Sage Plain, of the vast Mesa Verde archaeological region, and of the much larger San Juan River Basin.

If the people of the ancient Pueblo communities could have seen centuries into the future and known the story of Ackmen, it would have had a familiar ring. The ancients knew a lot about packing up their valuables and moving when times grew hard—when a drought hit or when the forests and game animals around their village became depleted. Sometimes, like the residents of old Ackmen, they merely shifted places within the area. Sometimes their migrations led them far away, with no return. Modern farm communities now overlie the ancient ones, but for all their manifest differences, the two peoples resemble each other in more ways than we might credit. They both knew about abandoned trash heaps, about deserted house foundations overgrown by sage.

## Chapter two

# *Twelve Thousand Years in the San Juan Country*

*Perhaps the most interesting ruins of America are found in this region. The ancient pueblos found here are of superior structure.... Wherever there is water, near by an ancient ruin may be found; and these ruins are gathered about centers, the centers being larger pueblos and the scattered ruins representing single houses. The ancient people lived in villages, or pueblos, but during the growing season they scattered about by the springs and streams to cultivate the soil by irrigation, and wherever there was a little farm or garden patch, there was built a summer house of stone.*

—John Wesley Powell
*Canyons of the Colorado*, 1895[1]

# June 20, 1997

The sky, lit by a low, full moon above the Great Sage Plain in the west, brightens slowly. The Rico Mountains, marking the spot where the summer solstice sun will rise, are silhouetted against the northeastern horizon. A chill breeze stirs a flock of jays into noisy protest in a grove of piñon and juniper trees not far down the slope from where I stand. Five sleek mule deer emerge from the shadows and turn to face the east, as if waiting with me to see the sun appear. At 6 a.m. the golden moon touches the earth in the west and a blinding sliver of sun slides up from the mountains in the east. The sun rises as the moon sets. For an instant the universe seems suspended in perfect balance. Then day begins.

I have come here today especially to watch the solstice sun rise as the full moon sets, an event that occurs only once every 19 years. But I come here often at any hour of the day, drawn more by the vistas sweeping in all directions than by any particular natural event. I am standing on the ridge that divides the San Juan River Basin from the Dolores River Basin in southwestern Colorado. Four hundred feet directly below me to the north is McPhee Reservoir on the Dolores. To the south the land slopes gently into the San Juan Basin. Ten miles away Mesa Verde and Sleeping Ute Mountain dominate the southern horizon. Through a gap between the two, I can see across the valley of the San Juan itself to the Chuska Mountains which lie along the border between New Mexico and Arizona. Near the Rico Mountains in the northeast are the 14,250-foot summits of the Wilson Mountains, marking the headwaters of the Dolores and the highest point in the Dolores Basin. The Abajo Mountains rise in the northwest from the rim of the San Juan Basin in Utah. The Great Sage Plain stretches away to the west. A quarter-mile away is a knoll topped by a twelfth-century pueblo.

That ruin was first recorded in 1776 by the Dominguez–Escalante expedition and visited again in 1859 by the Macomb expedition. Professor J.S. Newberry described the pueblo and the view from the knoll in his 1876 report on the Macomb expedition:

> From the summit of the hill...we obtained a magnificent view of a wide extent of country lying on every side of us. In the east the Sierra de la Plata rose as a high and unbroken wall,

presenting a more varied outline than when seen from the other side; south of the Sierra, the *puerta* through which we had passed; beyond this, stretching far off southward, the green slopes and lofty battlements of the Mesa Verde beetling over the plain like some high and rock-bound coast above the level ocean; south, and near us, the miniature peak and chain of La Late; far more distant, the Sierras Carriso and Tunecha in the Navajo country; occupying the whole western horizon the monotonous expanse of the Sage-plain, beyond which rose the low summits of the Orejas del Oso, Sierra Abajo, and Sierra la Sal. In the north appeared a new and grand topographical feature...a chain of great mountains, higher and more picturesque than any we had seen.... One of the mountains in this group bears a large surface of snow, and its height cannot be less than 13,000 feet. Several others are nearly as lofty, and are cones of great beauty.

 The hill from which we obtained this view is crowned with an extensive series of very ancient ruins. The principal one is a pueblo, nearly 100 feet square, once substantially built of dressed stone, now a shapeless heap, in which the plan of the original structure can, however, be traced. Like most of the ruined pueblos of New Mexico, it consisted of a series of small rooms clustered together, like cells in a beehive. Near the principal edifice are mounds of stone, representing subordinate buildings.[2]

I am standing at an elevation of about 7,200 feet, near the upper limit of arable land in the San Juan Basin. From this vantage point I can see the small clusters of buildings, dwarfed in that expanse, marking the centers of several of the twentieth-century farming communities of the Great Sage Plain. Because I know where they are, I am also able to pick out the centers of a few of the Pueblo Indian farming communities that flourished for hundreds of years here until near the end of the thirteenth century. Modern communities overlie the ancient ones.

The San Juan Basin is on the Colorado Plateau. It is bordered on the east by the Rio Grande Basin, on the north by the Gunnison River and Dolores River basins, on the west by the Colorado River valley, and on the south by the Little Colorado River Basin. The basin is 240 miles long from east to west and, at its widest point, 150 miles from north to south. The San Juan River itself, which never follows the shortest distance between two points, runs 350 miles from its headwaters to the place, now submerged by Lake Powell, where it enters the Colorado.

The San Juan Basin encompasses 25,000 square miles, roughly the size of West Virginia, or Switzerland and Israel combined, and is as ecologically diverse as those two nations are from each other. There is a drop of nearly two vertical miles from the top of the highest mountain peak to the point where the San Juan enters the Colorado. The highest elevations in the basin, from 12,000 feet to more than 14,000 feet, are above timberline and as treeless as the arctic tundra which they resemble in climate and vegetation. From timberline, the land plunges through dense alpine forests of spruce, fir, and aspen, then evens out across the piñon and juniper forests of the fertile central mesas, and drops again to the rock-ribbed basin floor, an arid region as bare as the mountaintops. It is too cold for trees to grow above timberline and too dry for them in the lower elevations. Precipitation ranges from more than 60 inches at the highest levels to less than six at the lowest. A frost-free growing season is virtually nonexistent in the mountains, but exists for more than half

One of the many deep canyons that cut through the Great Sage Plain. The area was home to ancestral Pueblo Indians for more than 1,000 years.
© Walter BigBee, *Comanche*, 2001.

the year in the lowest basin.

Farms survive only in the temperate, mid-elevation regions—caught between the cold, wet high country and the hot, dry basin floors. The boundaries of the moderate regions do not hold; they fluctuate unpredictably. Floods one year can be followed by drought the next. An early summer this year might be followed by a long winter next year. Deciding when it's safe to plant tender crops such as beans and corn is a guessing game at best. Once they've sprouted, ensuring they get the water and warmth necessary to produce a good harvest is a matter left to prayer.

The histories of modern communities in the basin are tied to the elevations at which they are located. At the highest are the mining camps and ghost towns founded in the late nineteenth century, when prospectors for gold and silver rushed into the San Juans as they were being wrested from the Ute Indians. In the forests are the lumber towns created by the need for boards to build the mining industry. Not far downstream are the farming communities that sprang up to feed the prospectors and lumberjacks. Finally, at the lowest elevations are many of the American Indian communities whose citizens now occupy the regions no one else wanted.

*Between the Little Colorado and the Rio San Juan there is a vast system of plateaus, mesas, and buttes, volcanic mountains, volcanic cones, and volcanic cinder cones. Some of the plateaus are forest-clad and have perennial waters and are gemmed with lakelets. The mesas are sometimes treeless, but are often covered with low, straggling, gnarled cedars and piñons, trees that are intermediate in size between the bushes of sage in the desert and the forest trees of the elevated regions. On the western margin of this district the great Navajo Mountain stands, on the brink of Glen Canyon, and from its summit many of the stupendous gorges of the Colorado River can be seen. Central in the region stand the Carrizo Mountains, the Lukachukai Mountains, the Tunitcha Mountains, and the Chusca Mountains, which in fact constitute one system, extending from north to south in the order named. These are really plateaus crowned with volcanic peaks.*

—John Wesley Powell
***Canyons of the Colorado,* 1895**

The first official European explorers—members of Coronado's expedition in 1540—skirted the southern edges of the San Juan Basin. The first Spanish settlers arrived in the Rio Grande Basin, just across the Continental Divide, later in the same century. In 1598, nearly a quarter-century before the Mayflower landed at Plymouth Rock, they established the first provincial capital of New Mexico on the outskirts of what is now called San Juan Pueblo. In 1610, the capital was moved to Santa Fe.

The San Juan Basin lay well within the Province of New Mexico. At the time the first capital was founded, the area was the domain of the Ute in the north and the Navajo in the south. Spanish colonists did not establish permanent communities in the basin, but traders and prospectors regularly entered Ute lands despite colonial laws forbidding them to do so. By the time of the first official Spanish exploration of the basin in 1765—the Rivera Expedition—many landforms, from mountain peaks to rivers, bore Spanish names, the same names many of them are known by today. Rivera and his Indian guides followed long-established trails north of the San Juan. In 1776, the Dominguez–Escalante expedition followed Rivera's route across the northern tributaries of the river and the Great Sage Plain in search of a route from Santa Fe to the newly founded missions in California. They turned back well before reaching their destination, but the route, the Spanish Trail, was still in use a few decades later. In 1825, the Province of New Mexico and the San Juan Basin became part of newly independent Mexico. In 1848, much of New Mexico, including the basin, was ceded to the United States as part of the Treaty of Guadalupe-Hildago that ended the war with Mexico. The first U.S. exploration of the basin in 1859, the Macomb Expedition, followed the old Spanish Trail.

In 1864, Kit Carson was ordered to remove the Navajo from their traditional domain south of the San Juan and forced them on the Long Walk to Bosque Redondo on the Pecos River in New Mexico Territory. A handful escaped north across the river where, according to local tradition, their descendants live today in and around the communities of Aneth and Montezuma Creek. In 1868, the Navajo were allowed to return to a much smaller reservation. Most of the Navajo Reservation now lies south of the San Juan in New Mexico, Arizona, and Utah, with the exception of a small area north of the river in the vicinity of Aneth and Montezuma Creek.

The original Ute domain covered all of what is now Colorado and much of Utah. An 1868 treaty relegated the Ute to the western half of Colorado, including the area in the basin north of the San Juan. In 1873, the Brunot Agreement took the higher elevations of the basin in Colorado from the Ute and opened it to prospectors who rushed into the mountains in search of gold and silver. In 1881, a final "agreement" consigned the Ute to two small reservations in Colorado along the New Mexico border and to one in Utah.

Today more than 50 percent of the land area of the San Juan Basin lies within five Indian reservations including the entire Ute Mountain Ute and Southern Ute reservations,

**Members of the Ute Capote band with a local settler, 1911. From left: Sue Williams, Dorcas Williams, John Bryce, and Price Williams.** Photographed by George Eggleston. Courtesy of La Plata County Historical Society.

*In the 1930s, archaeologists began referring to the ancient farming peoples of the San Juan Basin as the Anasazi, a Navajo word meaning "ancient ones" or "ancient enemies." I have had several conversations recently with individuals from pueblos who have asked that I refer to them in the way in which they refer to themselves. A scholar from Jemez refers to his people as* Hemish. *A Zuni told me he is* Shiwi, *and his people, collectively, are* A:shiwi. *A Hopi objects to the use of "Anasazi" in describing his ancestors and asks that I use* Hisatsinom *instead. He objects, too, to the term "prehistoric," asserting that the history of his people is well known to them.*

*As a resident of the Four Corners country, I find myself in sympathy with these requests to call people and places by their proper names. As a writer, I am sometimes perplexed over how to communicate the meaning of indigenous terms to readers who are unfamiliar with them. I recently completed a manuscript on local archaeological sites in which I avoided any use of the terms "Anasazi" and "prehistoric"—both of which have very specific, universal meanings for archaeologists. I circulated the manuscript among veteran Southwestern archaeologists, expecting to be criticized for not using those terms. I got plenty of constructive criticism, but not once was it suggested that I use either of the offending terms. That makes me think that the transition to a more indigenous terminology might be easier than I expected.*

—Ian Thompson
"Four Corners Almanac"[3]

large parts of the Jicarilla Apache and Navajo reservations, and a thin slice of the Hopi Reservation. The Jicarilla Apache were moved from their traditional homeland elsewhere in New Mexico in 1890. No Hopi have permanent homes in the area of their reservation lying within the basin. Roughly 12 percent of the basin land area is privately owned, and the balance is public land administered by the United States Forest Service, the Bureau of Land Management, and the National Park Service. About half the population of the basin now comprises members of the four American Indian cultures who call it home. Anglos —those who are neither American Indian nor Hispanic—are the second largest group. Hispanics, descended from the earliest European settlers in New Mexico, are the smallest ethnic group.

Archaeologists do not know how long Navajos have lived in the San Juan Basin, though they believe these people came from the area that today is interior Alaska and northwestern Canada, where tribes speaking closely related languages still live. The earliest known Navajo archaeological sites contain wood that dates to the early sixteenth century, but the Navajo believe they were here well before that time and that they, in fact, emerged into this world in the San Juan Basin itself. Neither is it known when the first Ute peoples arrived. The oral tradition of at least one Hopi clan contains references to Ute people in the basin at the time the Hopi were living there, which means the Ute were here before the end of the thirteenth century at the latest.

Of the several hundreds of thousands of archaeological sites in the basin, most date to the time before the first white settlers entered the area in the late nineteenth century. The sites form an *archaeological record*, and through its study archaeologists glean information about past inhabitants and the changes that occurred within cultural groups through time. The archaeological record is also a source of data on prevailing climatic and ecological conditions at any point in past time.

It is possible to learn something about a particular archaeological site simply by examining artifacts lying exposed on the modern ground surface. Much more can be learned by carefully excavating a site to reveal the artifacts that have been buried over time beneath layers of wind- or water-deposited soil. Only a small percentage of the sites in the San Juan Basin have ever been seen by archaeologists and far fewer—less than 1,000—have been excavated. The inescapable consequence of this glaringly incomplete body of information is that archaeologists cannot answer with certainty specific questions about the past. If asked, for instance, when the first corn was planted in the basin, an archaeologist can only reply with the age of the oldest corn excavated. He knows it is possible that corn centuries older than that may be contained in an unexcavated site elsewhere. Because the introduction of corn into ancient economies triggered profound changes in the cultures that accepted it, the time when those changes began remains as uncertain as the age of the oldest corn. One archaeologist refers to this as the "intrinsic ambiguity of the archaeological record." The record is not ambiguous, but what we know about it is.

The earliest known archaeological site in the San Juan Basin is about 12,000 years old. It is a temporary *Paleo-Indian* campsite left behind by a small band of people who relied almost solely upon their hunting skills to survive. They, and other bands like them, pursued mammoths and large bison over vast expanses extending from the Great Plains to the Great Basin during the chilly and moist Late Ice Age. They were a truly mobile people, rarely pausing anywhere for any length of time.

As the Ice Ages ended and the climate slowly warmed and became drier, the largest mammals vanished. By 8,000 years ago the climate—and the plant and animal life—more closely resembled that in the San Juan Basin today. There are more known archaeological sites dating to the *Archaic* period than to the earlier period. As with the earlier sites, these are temporary camps, but they appear to have been occupied longer or revisited during particular seasons. The shift from Paleo-Indian to the Archaic was as gradual as the warming and drying of the climate.

One significant difference between the two was that the small bands of Archaic people did not range nearly as far in their pursuit of food. The wide-ranging mammoths and large bison were gone by then. Elk, deer, mountain sheep, smaller mammals, and birds provided much of the protein in the Archaic diet. The annual migration routes of elk and deer were relatively localized. In late spring and summer, they ascended into the mountains. Later in the year, they descended to winter feeding grounds on the mesas. As the Archaic bands followed the game, they gathered mountain plants in the summer and in spring and autumn collected plants near their winter camps on the lower mesas.

This mobile way of life is the *seasonal round*, and the people who practice it are *hunter–gatherers*. The San Juan Basin, with its rapid elevational transitions from tundra above timberline to basin grasslands with forests sandwiched in between, could sustain a seasonal round for small bands of hunter–gatherers.

This way of life was by no means unique to this area. Until the dawn of agriculture roughly 10,000 years ago, all humans were hunters and gatherers. Measured against more than a million years since the origin of the human genus, agriculture is new and represents a mere tick of the cultural clock. Hunter–gatherers still exist in some parts of the world, and the particulars vary from culture to culture.

Studies of the archaeological record throughout the world show that the shift from hunting and gathering to agriculture rarely occurs rapidly. As the dependence on domestic crops grows, the reliance on hunting and gathering diminishes. One of the most significant consequences of this shift is that residential patterns change from mobile, with frequent

**The Hayden Survey mapping in the Great Sage Plain in 1874.** Photo courtesy of Colorado Historical Society (10028084).

moves from camp to camp, to sedentary, with homes in permanently established settlements near fields. Recent research by the Crow Canyon Archaeological Center in the ancient farming regions of the Great Sage Plain demonstrates that this polarized "either/or" stereotyping of hunting and gathering versus farming residential practices is an exaggerated oversimplification that actually conceals important information necessary to understanding the household and social organization of farming societies.

Corn was probably the first domestic crop grown in the San Juan Basin. Until recently, it was thought that corn was not introduced into the area until just a few hundred years B.C. A new technique of radiocarbon dating using an accelerator mass spectrometer, *AMS dating*, requires only tiny samples of carbon so that individual corn kernels can now be dated. Using this technique, archaeologists date corn from sites in the Chinle Valley of New Mexico and the Marsh Pass area of Arizona to between 1000 and 1500 B.C.

Whenever it occurred, the dawn of agriculture in the San Juan Basin signaled the approach of profound changes in the way many of the inhabitants of the region lived. By 2,200 years ago, houses—which may have been occupied only during growing seasons— were regularly being built in the middle elevations of the basin, where farming conditions are most favorable. These *pit structures* were partly underground, with the tops of the walls and roofs extending above ground level. Variations on these structures were part of the architecture of the basin for the next 1,500 years, until the people migrated into the adjacent Little Colorado and Rio Grande drainages.

Though they became larger and more livable over time, pit structures remained the sole form of residential architecture for many centuries. The *Basketmaker Phase* of Southwestern culture is named for the beautifully woven baskets found in association with this architecture. Pottery making did not begin until about A.D. 500, long after the appearance of the first pit houses. By about 700, people began to build residential and storage structures entirely above ground, although pit structures continued to be an important part of every residence and settlement. The centuries following the construction of the first aboveground dwellings are the *Pueblo Phase* of ancient farming cultures. It would be 150 years after the beginning of the Pueblo Era before construction began at Pueblo Bonito, a massive stone building that eventually reached a height of five stories, in what is now Chaco Culture National Historical Park. Another 300 years after that, construction began on Cliff Palace in Mesa Verde National Park.

The larger aboveground stone buildings—most of which crumbled into mounds of rocky rubble—and the cliff dwellings caught the eye of the first European and U.S. explorers and mappers of the region. Escalante noted the ruins and their resemblance to the pueblos along the Rio Grande in his 1776 journals, and almost 100 years later, Professor J.S. Newberry, chronicler of the 1859 Macomb Expedition, did the same. In 1874, William Henry Jackson—already famous for his photographs of the wonders of Yellowstone—left the Hayden Survey in Silverton, Colorado, high in the San Juans, to photograph the cliff dwellings of Mancos Canyon in Mesa Verde and the exquisite stone towers of McElmo Canyon. By the mid-1880s, recently arrived white settlers were systematically looting the ruins—particularly ancient burial sites—for their beautiful pottery and other artifacts. By the turn of the twentieth century, there were few undesecrated ruins off-reservation.

Scholarly archaeological research began at several locations in the San Juan Basin in the late nineteenth and early twentieth centuries. Mesa Verde National Park was created in 1906 to protect the spectacular cliff dwellings located there, and in the next two decades, several additional national monuments were created to protect some of the largest or most visually appealing ancient buildings in the basin. The creation of the national park and national monuments focused most archaeological research within their boundaries. It was easier to find public and private funding to conduct expensive research within Park Service preserves than outside them.

*North of the Rio San Juan another vast plateau region is found, stretching to the Grand River. The mountains of this region are the La Plata Mountains, Bear River Mountains, and San Miguel Mountains on the east, and the Sierra El Late, the Sierra Abajo, and the Sierra La Sal on the west…. Throughout the region mountains, volcanic cones, volcanic necks, and coulées are found, while the mountains themselves rise to great altitudes and are forest-clad. Some of the plateaus attain huge proportions, and between the plateaus labyrinthian mesas are found. Buttes, as stupendous cameos, are scattered everywhere, and the whole region is carved with canyons.*

—John Wesley Powell
**Canyons of the Colorado, 1895**

**The Cliff Palace in Mesa Verde National Park.** Photo courtesy of Colorado Historical Society (10028076).

Buildings and pottery are among the most durable of ancient Puebloan creations, and architectural and pottery styles and technology changed through time and across space. By the 1930s, archaeologists working in the San Juan Basin, often on sites in national park lands, identified three regions and cultural groups based on variations in architectural and pottery styles. The Chaco archaeological region in New Mexico is contiguous with the Chaco River drainage south of the San Juan and east of the Chuska Mountains, and is linked to the architectural and pottery styles found in the Chaco Culture National Historical Park. The Kayenta archaeological region in Arizona, where Canyon de Chelly and Navajo national monuments (and the Navajo town of Kayenta) are located, is roughly contiguous with the Chinle Wash drainage west of the Chuskas and south of the San Juan. The Mesa Verde archaeological region comprises most of the San Juan Basin north of the river in Colorado and New Mexico. A fourth recently recognized region, the Totah, is along the San Juan in New Mexico and exhibits architectural and pottery styles found in the Chaco region before 1150 and in the Mesa Verde region after that.

Ancient "roads," some stretching for miles, were first found in the Chaco region. More recently, similar and shorter "roads" were found in the Mesa Verde region. The "roads," and the presence of Chaco-style architecture and pottery in the Mesa Verde region, led to a hotly debated archaeological issue: Was there a Chacoan "empire" or "system" extending throughout the basin and beyond between the years 1050 and 1150? That debate is likely to continue for a long time before it is resolved.

The Mesa Verde region covers more than 10,000 square miles, an area the size of Maryland. Mesa Verde National Park, for which the region is named, covers a mere 52 square miles. Much of the terrain is mountainous and above arable elevations. The deepest and most fertile soils are found in the central portion of the region, which is dominated by the canyon-cut tableland known as Mesa Verde, and the Great Sage Plain to the north and west.

Although there are many times more Puebloan sites on the Great Sage Plain than on all of Mesa Verde, archaeological research focused on the park proper for much of the twentieth century, resulting in stabilized sites open to the public and technical reports designed for the professional archaeologist. Jesse W. Fewkes' early excavations at

Cliff Palace, Spruce Tree House, and the Far View Complex focused on the late Pueblo periods. In the 1940s and early 1950s, James Allen Lancaster and others excavated late Basketmaker and early Pueblo sites that now form the famous Ruins Road displays. The extensive Wetherill Mesa Project of the late 1950s and early 1960s supported Alden Hayes, James Lancaster, and Arthur Rohn's groundbreaking research on settlement patterns and community organization. Concurrently, and extending through the middle 1970s, Robert Lister, David Breternitz, and Jack Smith directed University of Colorado archaeological field schools and produced reports on a variety of sites.

By contrast, no large-scale archaeological research took place on the Great Sage Plain for the 40 years following Paul S. Martin's completion of field research in the Ackmen–Lowry area in 1938. College and university field schools continued to conduct research at a few sites. In the 1970s, Wichita State University conducted research in the McElmo drainage under the direction of Arthur Rohn. Escalante Pueblo was excavated under the guidance of University of Colorado professor David Breternitz, who became principal investigator for the Dolores Archaeological Project shortly thereafter. This project is an example of *cultural resource management.* This type of archaeology—mandated by legislation whenever development on federal lands, or development undertaken with federal funding, will disturb the archaeological record—began gaining momentum throughout the central Mesa Verde region in the late 1970s.

Though it is technically not in the San Juan Basin nor on the Great Sage Plain, the massive Dolores Archaeological Project got underway in the adjacent Dolores River Valley in 1978. The initial goal of the project was to study the archaeological record in a 10-mile-long segment of the valley that would soon be inundated by McPhee Reservoir, to be created to store water needed to irrigate thousands of acres on the Great Sage Plain. A later phase of the project would study the parts of the archaeological record of the Great Sage Plain that would be destroyed when irrigation canals and pipelines snaking out from the reservoir were constructed. Scores of archaeologists were part of the almost two-decade-long, multimillion-dollar project.

Immediately following its establishment in 1982, the Crow Canyon Archaeological Center began field research on the Great Sage Plain, initiating the longest-lived research program ever undertaken in the Mesa Verde region. In formulating and presenting their research results, Crow Canyon archaeologists draw heavily on research conducted by the Dolores Archaelogical Project, by archaeologists who have worked in the region and the entire San Juan Basin since the late nineteenth century, and by archaeologists and ethnographers working in similar societies throughout the world. New information about the central Mesa Verde region—some of it challenging conventional archaeological wisdom—is emerging from this research. Just as significantly, the Center developed new methods for answering questions about the archaeological record, and refined existing methods. Current designs will guide Crow Canyon's research in the first decade of the twenty-first century.

Standing on the ridge where I went to observe the moon set and the sun rise on the summer solstice in 1997, I can look down on McPhee Reservoir and the Dolores River Valley. I can turn and look into the San Juan Basin sloping away from my feet. Ever since I was a child, I have been visiting the ancient Puebloan buildings here. Only recently, however, have I seen those buildings as the material remnants of communities, some of them with histories that spanned centuries. Much more remains to be learned, and that is what Crow Canyon's current research is designed to do. From this spot, I can see the land sloping gently down to the foot of Sleeping Ute Mountain. Most of the land between me and the mountain is now covered by agricultural fields interlaced with piñon and juniper forests that mark the untillable canyon rims. In one of those forested areas, 10 miles away, the land rises to form a slightly discernible knoll. On top of that knoll is a small ninth-century residential site, Duckfoot. Research at Duckfoot produced new information about the nature of ancient Pueblo culture and provided the foundation for Crow Canyon's later inquiries into the dynamics of the ancient farming communities of the Great Sage Plain.

# Chapter three

✳

## *Duckfoot*

## June 9, 1997

It is mid-afternoon. A thin layer of clouds obscures the sun, softening the shadows of the piñons and junipers surrounding the small clearing where we are standing. A breeze whispers in the trees. There is no other sound. The land falls away quickly toward Alkali Canyon in the west, more gradually through a thin strip of forest and then across a vast, gently rolling field toward Crow Canyon in the east. Visible at my feet are a few slabs of stone standing on edge and aligned east-to-west. These are the remnants of aboveground room walls at the Duckfoot site, a tiny hamlet where Puebloan farmers once lived. Immediately south of the walls lie four circular depressions, the only visible evidence of four pit houses inhabited more than 1,100 years ago.

When archaeologists E. Charles Adams and Bruce Bradley began fieldwork here in 1983 for the Crow Canyon Archaeological Center, head-high sage obscured the walls and depressions. Crews cleared the sage to make way for excavations. On the first day of digging, a crew member found a pottery duck's foot, giving Duckfoot its name. The second duck foot was found five years later, when excavation was nearly complete, but the duck itself was never found. After the digging was finished in 1987, the site was backfilled, or reburied, with the soil and stone removed earlier. Backfilling is the best

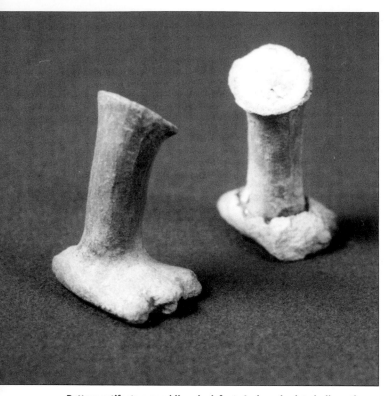

**Pottery artifacts resembling duck feet. Archaeologists believe these were supports for a duck-effigy vessel.** Photo by Rick Bell, © Crow Canyon Archaeological Center, 1993.

way to preserve an excavated site from damage by the elements. Duckfoot now looks the way it did before, except that the sage has not yet grown back.

I am with archaeologist Ricky Lightfoot, now president of the Crow Canyon Archaeological Center. Ricky assumed responsibility for field research at Duckfoot in 1985, and was assisted in the field by archaeologists Carrie Lipe and Mark Varien. Although it has been more than a decade since he completed the initial phase of research, Lightfoot still glances across the site as if he knows it like the back of his hand. He does. If asked how many pieces of broken pottery were unearthed at Duckfoot, Ricky responds instantly, "One hundred twelve thousand, one hundred ninety-seven." He has reason to remember.

Lightfoot is in his mid-forties, lanky, with pale blue eyes beneath a shock of dark hair. His face exhibits the creases seen on those who smile easily and often. He speaks softly with a faint East Texas accent. Nothing about his manner reveals the obsession with which he pursued research at Duckfoot.

Ricky came to southwestern Colorado in 1980 to work on the immense Dolores Archaeological Project conducted by the Bureau of Reclamation 10 miles north of Duckfoot. One of that project's goals was to study archaeological sites along the Dolores River that would later be flooded when a dam was built to create McPhee Reservoir. Many of the sites there dated to the ninth century, just as Duckfoot did. When he became director of the Duckfoot project, he designed his research to take advantage of the tremendous amount of information produced by the Dolores project. Did the conclusions reached in the Dolores research also apply to Duckfoot? Research at Duckfoot was important in its own right because the hamlet's life span immediately preceded the onset of major changes among the Puebloan people of the Mesa Verde region. The apparent drama that surrounded the abandonment of Duckfoot and other sites in the area may have been a precursor to those changes.

Described in the most basic terms, Duckfoot was a ninth-century farming hamlet of 19 aboveground rooms and four pit structures. Immediately south of the pit houses was the midden, the area where refuse such as fireplace ash, broken pottery, and discarded animal bone was left to decay back into the earth. It was also the place where the dead were buried. Strong archaeological evidence suggests that Puebloans of the Mesa Verde region considered middens special places. The layout of the site—the aboveground rooms on the north, the pit structures and courtyards just south of the rooms, and the midden south of the pit structures—was typical of residential sites in the region at the time. It was a pattern that would continue for the next four centuries, even through marked changes in architecture and building techniques. Duckfoot's founders began building in roughly 850, and the residents deserted their hamlet in about 880. Centuries later, archaeologists discovered in the pit houses the skeletons of seven people whose bodies were placed there at the end of occupation. Three of the pit houses and seven of the aboveground rooms burned at that time, hinting at a dramatic final day in the site's history.

The preceding brief descriptions required a total of five years of excavation to acquire. But the questions that most interested Ricky would take an additional six years in the laboratory to answer. He wanted to know, for example, not just the overall dates of the site but also when and in what sequence the aboveground rooms and pit structures were built. How long were individual structures used? Did some of them fall into disuse before the site was entirely abandoned? Formulating the questions themselves took time. Selecting or developing research methods that could be used to answer the questions took more.

Ricky's research at Duckfoot focused on ancient Puebloan households. We often use the term *household* today to mean a nuclear family of parents and children or an extended family that might include grandparents, aunts, uncles, and cousins. In some cases we are referring to people who live together but are not necessarily related to one another. In short, it isn't easy to define a household in today's world, much less in the world of more than 1,000 years ago. Ricky used the term to describe either nuclear or extended families living in a single residence.

In a modern American apartment building, each household inhabits a functional suite of rooms—bedrooms, living room, kitchen, bathroom—that is nearly identical to all the other suites in the building. By counting the number of residential suites, it is possible to determine the maximum number of households living in the apartment building. Was it possible, Ricky asked, to determine how rooms and structures at Duckfoot were used? If so, and if more than one nearly identical architectural suite existed there, could it be assumed that each was used by a separate household? Could he, therefore, determine the number of households that lived at Duckfoot? Could he even estimate the number of people who made it their home?

Each household occupying a modern apartment building has its own set of tools and utensils for daily use. That assemblage might include one vacuum cleaner, one broom, one dustpan, and one mop and mop bucket for cleaning floors, a complete set of cooking utensils for preparing meals, a complete set of dinnerware for use at mealtimes, one kitchen table, six kitchen chairs, and so forth. By identifying sets of such objects through-out an entire apartment building, future archaeologists might estimate the number of households that lived there. Looking at the past, Ricky asked: If more than one nearly identical assemblage of artifacts were found at Duckfoot, could it be assumed from such redundancy that each assemblage was used by a separate household? Would it be possible to use the number of sets of artifacts to estimate the number of households that once inhabited the hamlet? This information might then be compared to the answer to the same question reached by counting architectural suites.

Objects that people used during the life of a site often fail to survive in the archaeo-logical record. They might be taken to a new home when occupants move; they might disappear through decay or erosion; they might vanish into the hands of looters. How is it possible to account for "lost" artifacts when reconstructing artifact assemblages? Broken

Crow Canyon archaeologist Ricky Lightfoot working at Castle Rock Pueblo in 1991. Ricky currently serves as the President and CEO of the Crow Canyon Archaeological Center. © Kristin Kuckelman, 1991.

*Ongoing archaeological research, and as a writer I rely on a lot of it, can be pretty messy stuff. It's inconclusive, uncertain of itself, and ambiguous. The very best research literature, even when it is finished and off the press, retains that ambiguity. In contrast, most of the books about archaeology written for the general public tend to be very certain of themselves. They present chronological sequences in lockstep fashion, and they create the misimpression that we really do know what happened back then.*

*I call that latter kind of writing "storytelling in the ruins." I think it does a disservice to research archaeologists. And I know it cheats the lay public of the opportunity to understand how archaeological research is really done.*

—Ian Thompson
"Four Corners Almanac"[1]

cooking pots are less subject to natural destruction than are many other kinds of artifacts, and, it is safe to assume, people seldom take along pieces of broken cooking pots when they move. Studies show that there are fairly consistent ratios between types of objects used in Puebloan sites—for example, ratios of plain gray cooking pots to elaborately painted bowls. People were more likely to carry painted pots with them to new residences because those pots were more time-consuming to produce. Was it possible to determine how many cooking pots were used at Duckfoot throughout its history?

Could Ricky determine how many painted pots, if any, were taken away at the time of its abandonment?

Households living in modern apartment buildings do not always interact with one another, at least not regularly. Neighboring Pueblo households, however, were unlikely to have been isolated. Ricky wondered whether the artifact assemblages and architectural suites at Duckfoot, taken together, might tell how much interaction existed between the households.

The questions multiplied: Were the households at Duckfoot part of a larger community? If the inhabitants burned structures and left behind useful objects when they deserted the hamlet, what does that tell us about their long-term plans? Are there similarities between what happened here and what happened at the same time at other sites in the region, such as those in the Dolores River Valley?

Setting out to answer these questions, Ricky began by using both architecture and tree-ring dates to determine the chronological order in which aboveground rooms and pit houses at Duckfoot were built. The walls of several of the 19 aboveground rooms were formed of unshaped stones and mud. Other walls consisted of closely set, upright poles covered with mud. In either case, walls bonded or abutted to one another at the corners of rooms told Ricky whether several rooms had been built at once in a single building event, or whether particular rooms had been added onto an existing building. Where walls continued in a straight line and were bonded at the corners, he assumed that they had all been built as a unit. Where walls met but were not bonded, he assumed in most cases that the abutting walls had been added onto those that were bonded. Once all the rooms were excavated, Ricky examined the walls. Unless corner abutments indicated otherwise, he assumed that contiguous rooms of the same style were part of a single construction episode. He called rooms that were built as a single unit a *room suite*.

He also assumed, on the basis of his experience in the Dolores River Valley and research by other archaeologists at similar sites in the Southwest, that construction of room suites in a single episode did not happen independently of construction of a pit house. A great deal of soil is required to build the type of aboveground walls found at Duckfoot, and the digging of an underground pit structure would have provided it. Therefore, it seemed safe to assume that room suites and adjacent pit structures were built together.

Ricky referred to the combination of a room suite with a pit structure as an *architectural suite*. On examining the construction methods used in the aboveground rooms, he concluded that Room Suite 2—the center room suite—and the nearest pit structure, Pit Structure 2, were built first. Taken together, Room Suite 2 and Pit Structure 2 made up the earliest architectural suite. Sometime later, Room Suite 1 was added to the western end of Room Suite 2, and Room Suite 3 was added to the eastern end. These later room suites, along with Pit Structures 1 and 3, brought the total number of architectural suites to three. Pit Structure 4 was built late in the site's history and may not have been part of a larger architectural suite.

There were, then, three nearly identical architectural suites. If each sheltered a single household, then three households lived at Duckfoot at one time. But Ricky wasn't ready to assume that one architectural suite equaled one household. He wanted more evidence.

To find that evidence, Ricky looked next at how the people used the rooms and pit structures. He wanted to know whether each suite encompassed all the kinds of functional spaces that a complete household would need—recall the modern American apartment building. In assessing *room function*, archaeologists rely on what they see at the site they are excavating, the work of others who have studied similar ancient sites, and the work of those who do research in similar cultures today. Because many of the sites excavated as part of the Dolores Project dated to the same time period, Ricky was able to apply what he knew of findings there to what he saw at Duckfoot.

The aboveground rooms fell into two general categories: "living" rooms and "storage" rooms. In living rooms, people cooked and ate food, slept, and carried on other activities of daily life. Living rooms contained fireplaces for cooking and heating, and they held food-processing tools such as utensils for grinding corn. Living rooms also contained short-term storage places such as bins along the walls and pits dug into the floors where food and other perishables could be sealed away from moisture and vermin. Long-term storage rooms, where food was safeguarded for winter and times of drought, were virtually bare of pits or other features and could be entered only through living rooms.

When Ricky examined the three room suites, he found that each contained at least one room used for cooking, corn grinding, and short-term storage—that is, a living room—and several others used for long-term storage. In other words, the room functions were redundant from one suite to another, indicating that they had, indeed, been used by three separate households. In each case, the living room or rooms were located in the southernmost—front—row of rooms, and the storage rooms sat at the back, in the northernmost row.

Turning his attention to the pit structures, Ricky observed that each of those, too, contained a fireplace and areas used for cooking, corn grinding, and short-term storage. Each architectural suite, then, appeared to combine a room suite with a pit house used as a living space. And the whole architectural suite served as home to an individual household.

In addition to looking for fireplaces, bins, and other architectural features on the floors of individual rooms and pit structures, Ricky examined the artifacts found in the structures for clues to how they were used. He saw that certain types of artifacts and features regularly appeared together in particular rooms—fireplaces and cooking pots in food preparation rooms, for example. This discovery lent further support to his interpretation of room use.

Finally, Ricky looked for evidence of doorways between rooms in the aboveground suites. Doorways are seldom well preserved in the type of construction used at Duckfoot, so he inferred their locations by examining gaps in wall foundations. Sometimes the Puebloans covered their doorways with sandstone slabs, and the locations of these slabs in the ruins connoted the existence of additional doors nearby. The excavation crew found doorways between living and storage rooms *within* room suites, but there

**Dryland farmers of the Great Sage Plain often plow around unexcavated archaeological sites, preserving their study for future generations.**
© Walter BigBee, *Comanche*, 2001.

were no connections *between* room suites. This strengthened Ricky's conviction that each room suite, with its associated pit structure, served as home for a single household.

Simply by examining the surviving architecture, Ricky reached preliminary conclusions about the approximate sequence in which structures were built and how particular structures were used. But that did not tell him *when* they were built or precisely in what sequence—or when they were abandoned.

Archaeologists working in the Southwest are fortunate because tree-ring "calendars" have been developed for many parts of the region. Growing conditions vary from year to year, trees grow at different rates annually, and the widths of the rings representing each year's growth are different. By comparing wood found in an ancient site with the tree-ring calendar for that area, researchers can determine when the tree lived. And if the outermost, or most recent, ring is still present, the year in which the tree died—the *cutting date*—can be precisely pinpointed. Archaeologists always hope to find structures that burned at the time of their abandonment. The charring reduces the bacterial action that would otherwise destroy a roof beam or other datable wood.

But even the use of cutting dates is less straightforward than it sounds. Puebloan builders sometimes collected old, but still usable, wood from trees that had been dead for decades. The year the tree died was not the year it became a post or roof beam. When the thrifty Puebloans vacated their houses, they often salvaged old building materials, including roof beams, to reuse if they were building new residences nearby—in much the same way the residents of Ackmen moved their houses to New Ackmen in the twentieth century. When a large number of cutting dates cluster within a short time, archaeologists consider them to reflect an actual building date.

Because several structures at Duckfoot did burn at abandonment, Ricky's crew found hundreds of samples of datable wood. Altogether, excavators unearthed 375 tree-ring samples. Ricky sent the samples to the Laboratory for Tree-Ring Research at the University of Arizona in Tucson for dating, and happily, 194 of them had cutting dates. Using those dates, he confirmed his preliminary conclusion that Architectural Suite 2, consisting of a pit structure and eight rooms, was the first built at Duckfoot—in 857. The builders added Architectural Suite 1 soon thereafter, possibly in 858. Architectural Suite 3 came last, probably in 859. Pit Structure 4 was built separately in 873 and occupied for only a few years. The latest date in Architectural Suite 3—and the latest date for the site—was 876. Ricky concluded that the date of site abandonment was no earlier than 876, and it could have been as late as 880.

Tree-ring dates from wood used in repairing rooms and pit structures helped corroborate the date of the hamlet's demise. The posts and roof beams used in building the pit structures were easily damaged by insects and rotted by moisture, and the pit houses could be lived in for no more than 10 years without repair. Tree-rings showed that the pit structure in Suite 3 had been substantially remodeled in the 860s and again in the 870s. The latest tree-ring remodeling dates in Suites 1, 2, and 3 were 872 and 873. The latest date in Pit Structure 4 was 875. All these dates were consistent with an endpoint for the site of roughly 880.

But did the people desert every structure at once, or did they let some fall into disuse earlier in the hamlet's history? The Puebloans of the San Juan Basin frequently vacated individual structures within a residential complex before they left the complex as a whole. These structures often

*A couple of weeks ago I took a good friend, Tessie Naranjo of Santa Clara Pueblo, to a large, thirteenth-century pueblo near where I live. Tessie is descended from the people who once lived in this pueblo. My dog, Chaco, ran circles around us as we slogged through the mud and snow, descended the first low cliffs at the canyon's edge, and slid down the slope toward the higher cliff below. Atop the high cliff are D-shaped structures surrounded by a low enclosing wall. Cliff dwellings rise against the face of the cliff....*

*As soon as we got to the edge of the high cliff I began pointing out to Tessie everything I saw there. I told her how the placement of architectural features within the pueblo seemed to conform to similar patterns at some other sites I had been studying.*

*In my enthusiasm it took me a while to realize that Tessie was regarding me with a tolerant smile. Finally she said, "I can see that you are interested in such things. What interests me are the people. What were they doing? Where were their fields? Where did they get water? Where were they bringing their firewood from? I wonder if they were interested at all in what interests you? Did they think about these things or did they just build this pueblo? You have to look beyond the pueblo itself to understand the pueblo."*

*That last sentence was a familiar one. I had heard it many times from Rina Swentzell, Tessie's sister. It's a reminder that works. These places make sense only in a larger context. Tessie stood looking at the snowmelt seeping down the face of the cliff and dripping from an overhang. She pointed to where the ollas would have sat beneath the drips, catching the precious water. After that I let her lead the tour of the pueblo.*

—Ian Thompson
"Four Corners Almanac"[2]

became alternative middens. Excavation revealed that no refuse was placed in any of the structures during the life of the site. With only two exceptions, the collapsed roofs of the structures rested directly upon the floor, with no midden material in between. This implied that the structures had all been in use as living or storage spaces up to the time of abandonment.

Judging from the architecture and tree-ring samples alone, it seemed apparent that the hamlet was home to three separate households throughout most of its history, from the late 850s to about 880. Thousands of artifacts were removed from the site and taken to the Crow Canyon Archaeological Center's research laboratory during the five six-month field seasons it took to excavate Duckfoot. Analysis of those artifacts could not begin in earnest until excavation was complete. The artifacts had their own stories to tell.

One of the first challenges Ricky faced was not decoding the stories contained in the artifacts, but determining to what extent artifacts were displaced over the centuries within Duckfoot itself, and whether some even failed to survive. No single artifact alone has much to tell. It is the spatial relationships of artifacts to one another—assemblages —that have meaning. Which artifacts did people take with them when they left? Were others destroyed by natural forces? Or carried away by modern looters? From the artifacts remaining, could he reconstruct what the hamlet's complete tool kit—the total number and kinds of tools and utensils in use at any one time—might have looked like?

Ricky was aided in this task by the fact that Crow Canyon archaeologists and lay excavators had dug nearly 100 percent of the site—a rare luxury in any archaeologist's experience. He could be sure that virtually all artifacts in existence at Duckfoot had been uncovered.[3]

First, Ricky looked for evidence that natural forces might have removed artifacts from the site. He concluded that because the hamlet was located atop a ridge and on a very gentle slope, rain and snow had washed away little, if any, of the site. Windblown soil buried much of the pueblo, including walls and floors, helping to keep artifacts in place. However, burrowing rodents and growing tree roots, which could easily have shifted artifacts away from their original resting places, disturbed much of the site.

And what about looting? Although looting and collecting appeared less severe at Duckfoot than at neighboring sites, some artifacts had certainly been lost that way. Two looter's pits were evident, and people living in the area said that some artifacts lying on the ground had been carried away. Among those items was a pottery duck—perhaps the one that stood on the two duck feet that gave the site its name. Still, Ricky could feel confident that relatively few of the buried artifacts had been lost.

With this general picture of how an artifact inventory might change over time, Ricky was ready to begin figuring out the makeup of the household tool kit. Among the artifacts filling bags and boxes on Crow Canyon's laboratory shelves were 42 metates—large stone slabs, some of them incised with troughs, on which corn and other seeds were placed for grinding into meal—and 38 manos, the rounded, hand-held stones used to do the grinding. There were hammerstones, polishing stones, axes, mauls, spear and arrow points, pottery effigies, pendants, beads, shell bracelets, awls, and gaming pieces. But it was potsherds, pieces of broken pots, that made up the vast bulk of the artifact inventory. And so it was to pottery that Ricky turned his attention.

Three categories of pottery made up the 112,197 potsherds found at Duckfoot: gray ware, white ware, and red ware. Local potters made the gray ware. It was ordinary, unpainted, unpolished pottery—mostly jars—which people put to many daily uses, including cooking and food and water storage. Of the three categories, gray ware required the least investment of labor to make, and it made up about 90 percent of the pottery unearthed. White ware, too, was made locally. Slipped, polished, and frequently decorated with designs in black paint, it was used for more specialized purposes, including serving cooked food, in some cases at feasts or during other ceremonial occasions. It made up 5 percent of all potsherds at Duckfoot. The balance, 5 percent, was red and imported, archaeologists believe, from southeastern Utah. Red ware was polished and usually painted. A good deal of labor went into making the pots and transporting them carefully many miles across a rugged landscape.

There were a great variety of types of gray ware pottery found at Duckfoot: small, medium, and large cooking jars; ollas (pronounced *oy-yas*) used for storing food and water; miniature jars; seed jars; and bowls. It was the cooking pots that interested Ricky most. If he knew how many cooking pots were used throughout the quarter century that Duckfoot was inhabited, it would be a big step toward determining the composition of the day-to-day tool kit. That was particularly true if he could figure out how many cooking pots were in use at any one time.

There is a remarkable consistency between the circumference of a cooking pot's rim and the overall size of the pot. Pots with small rim circumferences are small pots (though one must be careful not to confuse them with ollas, which are much larger but also have small mouths). Pots with large rim circumferences are large pots. There is a continuous range of sizes between small and large cooking pots, but Ricky generalized the sizes for Duckfoot into "small," "medium," and "large."

The first method used to estimate the total number of cooking pots was to sort through more than 65,000 potsherds from a selected part of the midden, looking for pieces of broken rims. Rim sherds that were large enough to be measured—2,348 of them—were matched to a chart depicting progressively larger concentric circles. These provided an accurate estimate of the circumference of the rim from which the sherd came and the percentage of the rim included in each sherd. The researchers determined that the portion of the midden selected for study yielded the rims of 75 pots, including six small, 49 medium, and 20 large cooking jars. From this, Ricky estimated that there were 206 broken and discarded pots in the midden. This number did not include whole or still-usable pots that people left inside rooms and pit structures when they abandoned the site.

To double-check the estimated totals, researchers separated the potsherds from the studied area of the midden into the various types of vessels and then weighed the sherds from each type. The ratio of rim to vessel size is consistent, and pots of a particular size are also of a consistent weight. Ricky confirmed that the estimate of total pots arrived at from rim circumferences was relatively accurate. He went on to estimate the number of cooking pots found in almost all contexts at Duckfoot, not just in the part of the midden under study. He came up with a total of 306 cooking pots—134 small, 123 medium, and 49 large.

But how many cooking jars of each size were in use at Duckfoot at any one time? Archaeologists and anthropologists working in the Southwest and elsewhere are interested in how long clay pots last before they break and are discarded. Clay cooking pots are excellent candidates for these studies because they break at fairly predictable rates. People use them frequently and accidentally knock them about or drop them. The continual heating and cooling of the pots on open fireplaces subjects them to nearly constant thermal stress. Researchers developed fairly consistent estimates of how long pots of a particular size will last. Small cooking jars last an average of 1.2 years; medium-size cooking jars, 1.5 years; and large, about 3 years.

So far, Ricky had determined the total number of cooking pots at Duckfoot, the number of each of the three sizes of pots, and the average number of years that vessels of each size were used before they broke. Tree-ring dates established that the occupancy of Duckfoot spanned 25 years. By multiplying the number of pots in each size category by the number of years pots of each size typically lasted, and then dividing that figure by 25, Ricky arrived at an estimate of the number of each size cooking pot in use at any given time: on average, 6.4 small pots, 7.4 medium pots, and 5.9 large pots.

Decades of research in the American Southwest enable archaeologists to arrive at predictable ratios of types of artifacts that can be expected to be found at a site—for example, ratios of metates to manos, pots to other tools, gray pots to white and red pots. Those predictions proved accurate at Duckfoot, except that there were fewer white and red pots relative to gray pots than was expected. Fewer of the large ollas appeared than were predicted as well. White ware and red ware pots were probably used more for special purposes than were gray ware pots, and they certainly were more time consuming to produce. Consequently, people had more reason to take them along when they moved away. And they might have needed large ollas to transport food to their new homes. Ricky concluded that this was probably what had happened to the missing pots and ollas.

At the end of his meticulous study of cooking pots, Ricky thought about his earlier conclusion that three separate households had lived at Duckfoot. Was there anything about the artifacts that would either support or contradict that conclusion? He looked at the artifacts found in each of the three architectural suites, reckoning that if a household occupied each suite, then each should contain all the artifacts required to meet basic subsistence needs. That proved to be the case. There were three fairly similar artifact assemblages, each associated with an architectural suite, which supported the three-household conclusion.

There was little evidence in the architecture proper to indicate the kinds of interaction among the three households. The three above-ground room suites were separated from each other by walls with no doorways, although rooms within individual room suites were connected. Might something in the artifact assemblages provide evidence of interaction among the households?

Ricky devised a method of using broken pots to look for household interaction. Duckfoot's residents did not discard every piece of broken pottery into the midden. Sometimes they kept large potsherds and put them to new uses. These large, recycled potsherds, called *sherd containers*, may have served as dippers, spoons, small bowls or, if they were large enough and shaped appropriately, even as cooking utensils.

Ricky limited his search to the seven living rooms in the aboveground block and to the four pit structures. He examined only those sherd containers found directly on the floors or on top of the fallen roofs (Puebloan people often worked on rooftops), the places sherd containers were most likely to be during occupancy. Ricky thought it possible that households living in different architectural suites might exchange sherd containers. Moreover, if a single parent pot produced more than one container, then those sherds might be in more than one architectural suite. If so, they would provide evidence of interaction between households. But the two sherd containers would have to fit together in order to confirm that they came from a single parent pot.

As it turned out, seven large sherds found in aboveground rooms fit together with seven large sherds found in pit structures. Two of them found in Architectural Suite 1 fit sherds from the pit structure in Architectural Suite 2. In addition, two large sherds in Pit Structure 1 fit two sherds in Pit Structure 2, one sherd from Pit Structure 2 fit a sherd in Pit Structure 4, and one sherd from Pit Structure 4 fit a sherd found in Pit Structure 3. Ricky established that there was interaction between Duckfoot's architectural suites and thus between the households occupying them.

**The Cliff Palace in Mesa Verde National Park.** Photo courtesy of Colorado Historical Society (10028076).

what is now Chaco Culture National Historical Park. Another 300 years after that, construction began on Cliff Palace in Mesa Verde National Park.

The larger aboveground stone buildings—most of which crumbled into mounds of rocky rubble—and the cliff dwellings caught the eye of the first European and U.S. explorers and mappers of the region. Escalante noted the ruins and their resemblance to the pueblos along the Rio Grande in his 1776 journals, and almost 100 years later, Professor J.S. Newberry, chronicler of the 1859 Macomb Expedition, did the same. In 1874, William Henry Jackson—already famous for his photographs of the wonders of Yellowstone—left the Hayden Survey in Silverton, Colorado, high in the San Juans, to photograph the cliff dwellings of Mancos Canyon in Mesa Verde and the exquisite stone towers of McElmo Canyon. By the mid-1880s, recently arrived white settlers were systematically looting the ruins—particularly ancient burial sites—for their beautiful pottery and other artifacts. By the turn of the twentieth century, there were few undesecrated ruins off-reservation.

Scholarly archaeological research began at several locations in the San Juan Basin in the late nineteenth and early twentieth centuries. Mesa Verde National Park was created in 1906 to protect the spectacular cliff dwellings located there, and in the next two decades, several additional national monuments were created to protect some of the largest or most visually appealing ancient buildings in the basin. The creation of the national park and national monuments focused most archaeological research within their boundaries. It was easier to find public and private funding to conduct expensive research within Park Service preserves than outside them.

> *North of the Rio San Juan another vast plateau region is found, stretching to the Grand River. The mountains of this region are the La Plata Mountains, Bear River Mountains, and San Miguel Mountains on the east, and the Sierra El Late, the Sierra Abajo, and the Sierra La Sal on the west…. Throughout the region mountains, volcanic cones, volcanic necks, and coulées are found, while the mountains themselves rise to great altitudes and are forest-clad. Some of the plateaus attain huge proportions, and between the plateaus labyrinthian mesas are found. Buttes, as stupendous cameos, are scattered everywhere, and the whole region is carved with canyons.*
>
> **—John Wesley Powell**
> ***Canyons of the Colorado,* 1895**

He next turned to cross-cultural studies to arrive at estimates for the sizes of the households. He found that, through time and across space, households averaged five to eight persons. Although in nineteenth- and twentieth-century Southwest pueblo households the range might be from 2 to 12 persons, the *average* is the standard 5 to 8. Judging from these figures, probably 15 to 24 people lived in the three households at Duckfoot at any one time.

Associated studies link household size to available square feet of living space. Modern pueblos average 17.7 square meters of roofed space per capita. Modern, year-round Navajo communities offer an average of 9.7 square meters per person. Duckfoot bore similarities to both. Its total of 242.4 square meters of roofed space would translate into a population of between 14 and 25. That is nearly identical to Duckfoot's estimated population based on average household sizes.

The households did not exist in isolation. They were part of a larger community. The terrain west of Duckfoot drops off steeply into Alkali Canyon. To the east, the land slopes gently toward Crow Canyon, two miles away. It is good farmland today, and was in the ninth century. Archaeologists who surveyed these farmlands found 11 other residential sites similar to Duckfoot. Judging from the kinds of pottery found on the surface, all of them were inhabited at approximately the same time. Just across Crow Canyon is a larger ninth-century site, Cirque Village, which probably housed 125 to 175 people. None of these other sites has been excavated.

*It is far too easy to dwell upon the departure of the Puebloan people, to ask why they left. Their farms, towns, and ceremonial centers are empty, silent, and overgrown. Their utensils are buried beneath centuries of windblown soil. What strikes us now is the sense of abandonment that clings to the ruins. And, somehow, in departure and desertion is connoted crisis and failure.*

*That isn't how we see the ruins of our own culture, whether they overlook Athens, surround Plymouth Rock, or are ghost towns perched high in the San Juan Mountains. They are seen by us as symbols of our success rather than our failure. We see them as mileposts on the way to where we are now. It does not occur to us to view the Puebloan ruins as guideposts to where we are now going in the place they called home.*

—Ian Thompson
"Four Corners Almanac"[4]

**Pottery vessels from the Duckfoot site excavation.** © Crow Canyon Archaeological Center, 1994.

Cirque Village and the surrounding 12 smaller sites, including Duckfoot, could have been part of a ninth-century community of more than 250 people. A *community* is a group of people who have regular, even daily, face-to-face contact with one another. The Cirque site might have been a community center. Lending support to that speculation is the probable existence of a large circular structure, a great kiva, capable of accommodating hundreds of people attending social, religious, or other community events. The great kiva would have been a focal point of community activity. At the same time that the Cirque community was farming land along Crow Canyon, similar but much larger villages and communities were farming the Dolores River Valley 10 miles north and nearly 1,000 feet higher.

I stood with Ricky on that June day in 1997 looking at the visible remains of Duckfoot. The double row of 19 rooms opened south onto the courtyards containing the four pit structures. Beyond them was the midden, where the dead were laid to rest. It was a quiet, peaceful place, once home to three ninth-century farm families for a quarter of a century. It was easy to envision the sights and sounds of children and pets playing in the courtyards while parents, grandparents, aunts, and uncles moved through the tasks of daily life—preparing food, mending and making tools, decorating pottery for firing, planting and harvesting, singing, gossiping, joking, and laughing. At dusk, as the sky darkened, families gathered in their own houses for the evening meal and to prepare for sleep. On special days, the three households might prepare a common feast to celebrate a successful hunt or a good harvest. At other times, perhaps they prepared food to take to Cirque Village where they visited with neighbors, feasted, and participated in ceremonies rooted in that place since time forgotten.

Why did life at Duckfoot end the way it did? Three of the four pit structures and seven of the aboveground rooms were deliberately burned at the time Duckfoot was deserted. Their collapsed roofs lay directly upon the floors, with no natural deposits between them, so Ricky knew they did not burn too long after the people left. Archaeologists working elsewhere in the Southwest already concluded that it would be difficult for a pit structure to catch fire accidentally, because so much of it consisted of earth. People would have to take large amounts of fuel into a pit house in order to build a fire hot enough to cause the roof to collapse.

The fires that burned the pit houses at Duckfoot generated intense heat that reddened the structure walls. According to Karen Adams, director of environmental archaeology at Crow Canyon, the fire in Pit Structure 1 was so hot that many plant parts left on the floor vitrified, becoming shiny and glasslike. The sides of rounded stems swelled and bubbled out in blisters. Some specimens believed to be resin globs became so hot that they turned liquid and then resolidified.

Because of the fires, Ricky was able to determine the season in which the people departed. On the floors of Pit Structures 1 and 3, excavators found abundant charred remains of sagebrush flower heads. Ricky believed that sagebrush was piled in the structures to fuel the fires. The flower heads had reached the stage of maturity found in September, and so he concluded that Duckfoot was abandoned in the fall.

Not only had much of the hamlet been burned, but the bodies of three men, two women, and two children had been carefully placed on the floors of the four pit structures before three of them were set ablaze. Contrary to contemporary Puebloan custom, there were no funeral items, such as pots, with the bodies. The collapsed roofs lay directly upon the skeletons, and Ricky determined that the bodies were placed on the floors at the time of abandonment.[5]

Analysis of the skeletons found in the pit houses and an additional seven found in the midden determined that all 14 individuals had been in reasonably good health. They were well nourished and suffered no diseases that left traces in the bones. Nor was there evidence that any died violently. It appeared unlikely that the surviving residents were forced by outsiders to abandon their homes. However, the close-spaced deaths of seven individuals—whatever the causes—may well have contributed to the survivors' decision to move away from the site and probably from the area.

Reasoning from all the evidence available, Ricky concluded that the final fires at Duckfoot were planned. The houses did not burn accidentally, and they were not hurriedly set afire at the height of a conflict with marauders. This fiery finale fit a pattern that emerged as data from excavations in the Dolores River Valley were analyzed. Many pit structures and some aboveground rooms there were burned when people left the valley for new homes elsewhere. A number of the Dolores pit structures, like those at Duckfoot, were converted into tombs.

Ricky interpreted the burning to mean that the departing inhabitants had no intention of returning. When they left, the people of Duckfoot were not moving a short distance to new homes elsewhere in the vicinity. If that had been the case, they would have salvaged many of the building materials for use in new construction. Because they left after harvest, when food supplies were abundant, they probably took pots used as storage containers to transport food. They also had to carry seeds with which to begin new farms. If the hamlet were abandoned in the spring, when stored food supplies were running low, more food containers would probably have been left behind.

The departing people took along their white ware and red ware pots, too—pots with greater aesthetic and sentimental value than the common gray ware cooking pots. But many, many items of daily life, items that would have to be fashioned anew on arrival at a distant destination, were left behind.

Taken together, the rich assortment of artifacts left at Duckfoot and the burning of the structures provide evidence that when they departed, the people were prepared for a long trip—and they had no intention of coming back.

During the 25 years that the three households of Duckfoot and all the other households of the Cirque community farmed the gentle slopes around Crow Canyon, at least 40 similar communities, many larger than Cirque, flourished in the Mesa Verde region. When, on that autumn day in the early 880s, the people of Duckfoot, carrying only a few treasured possessions, turned their backs on their burning homes and set off on a long journey, they may not have been traveling alone.

# Chapter four

# *Communities on the Move*

Long ago, ere the foot of the white man
    Had left its first print on the sod,
A people, both free and contented,
    Her mesas and cañon-ways trod.
Then Dolores, the river of sorrow,
    Was a river of laughter and glee,
As she playfully dashed through the cañons
    In her turbulent rush to the sea....

Gone, gone are this people forever,
    Not a vestige nor remnant remains
To gather the maize in its season
    And join in the harvest refrains;
But the river still mourns for her people
    With weird and disconsolate flow,
Dolores, the river of sorrow,
    Dolores—the river of woe

—Alfred Castner King, "Dolores,"
    *The Passing of the Storm
    and Other Poems*, 1907[1]

# August 14, 1997

The morning shadows are still long, but the air is warming rapidly in the heat of the summer sun. The birdsong and whispering breeze that greeted the day are gone now. The cool, glittering blue water in the valley below already looks inviting. By noon it will be almost irresistible. But I will have left this place by then.

I glance northwest at the Abajo Mountains on the edge of Utah's Great Sage Plain. I let my gaze follow the northern horizon in a great arc past Lone Cone, the Dolores Peaks, and the Wilson Mountains at the headwaters of the Dolores River, past La Plata Mountains in the east, and on south to Mesa Verde. I imagine, but cannot see, the La Plata River running south from among the mountains of that name, and the southward-flowing Animas River beyond that. Together, the Great Sage Plain, the La Plata River Valley, the Animas River Valley, and Mesa Verde itself make up most of the Mesa Verde archaeological region.

I am with Richard Wilshusen, who was director of research at the Crow Canyon Archaeological Center from 1993 to 1995. He is now a research associate of the Center, and he teaches anthropology at the University of Colorado, Boulder. We are sitting atop the ridge that separates the San Juan and Dolores river basins. Hidden beneath the deep waters just below us, where McPhee Reservoir flooded the Dolores Valley in the mid-1980s, are more than 900 archaeological sites, most of them dating to the ninth century.

Before the reservoir dam was built, the Bureau of Reclamation sponsored a massive study, the Dolores Archaeological Program, designed to glean as much data as possible about the archaeology of the Dolores Valley before it was flooded. Results from the project created an entirely new picture of life in the valley over a span of nearly three centuries, from 600 to 900. One archaeologist with the project estimated that the valley had a population of 3,000 or more in 880. Thirty years later, by the early tenth century, no one lived there at all.

Richard Wilshusen worked as an archaeologist with the Dolores project, and much of his research since then has focused on the movement of people to and from the valley in the ninth century, and to and from the Mesa Verde region as a whole over a longer time span. Why did they leave and where did they go? These questions still fascinate us as archaeological research in the Mesa Verde region enters the twenty-first century.

From where Richard and I sat, we could see the location of the Duckfoot hamlet and the Cirque village, both parts of the ancient Cirque community. They lay 1,000 vertical feet below us and 10 miles south. Ricky Lightfoot's research at Duckfoot focused on households. Richard Wilshusen, on the other hand, was interested in ninth-century villages. Where Ricky defined hamlets and villages in terms of numbers of rooms—fewer than 50 rooms equaled a hamlet; more than 50, a village—Richard defined them by population. A site or tight cluster of sites housing fewer than 100 persons was a hamlet. Sites or clusters of sites with populations ranging from 100 to 1,000 were villages. Both Richard and Ricky considered the Cirque site, with more than 50 rooms and some 125 to 175 people, a village. They referred to Cirque village, Duckfoot, and other hamlets in the vicinity, as the Cirque Community.

Both scholars considered communities to be clusters of households, hamlets, or villages located close enough to one another to allow their residents regular, face-to-face contact. Empty or sparsely populated terrain separated one community from the next. In the 1980s, these two criteria—regular contact among residents and discernible clustering of sites on the landscape—formed the accepted definition of ancient communities in the Mesa Verde region.[2] Sometimes a single village was large enough and isolated enough on the landscape to be considered a community in its own right.

Richard's research also addressed *settlement patterns*—the ways sites were situated on the landscape. Sometimes a community was composed simply of single households and small hamlets dispersed across a geographical area. Other communities encompassed a single, large, tight cluster of residential sites with no other sites in its vicinity. In rare cases, from Richard's perspective, a single, large site surrounded by a few dispersed sites made up the community. In all cases, the community's geographical boundaries enclosed farm-lands, woodlands, water supplies, and other resources needed to support its residents. Thus, a community could be a certain number of people residing closely together, or a geographical place on the landscape.

Richard's research confirmed earlier observations that the histories of some ancient Puebloan communities included phases when all of the population was dispersed within particular geographical community boundaries. Following these phases came times when the population joined together in large, aggregated villages, though they still controlled the same geographical boundaries that the dispersed population did. Richard established that the switch from dispersed hamlets to aggregated villages usually took place rapidly. What environmental or social forces triggered the transformation from dispersed to aggregated settlements? What did the residents of communities gain by coming together into villages? What was lost in the process?

To answer these questions, Richard began by doing a cross-cultural study of villages in 28 cultures throughout the world. All of them bore some resemblance to the Puebloan culture that once flourished in the Mesa Verde region and the San Juan Basin. Some of the patterns matched findings in the Dolores River Valley. For example, villages typically emerged in areas with low population densities; they were not a means of packing more people into a crowded landscape. The political or social organization of villages differed little from that in communities with dispersed settlement patterns. Richard found that many villages lasted no more than 25 years, and most houses in villages were lived in for an average of that long.

Once he had completed the cross-cultural study, Richard looked at two of the largest ninth-century villages in the valley—McPhee and Grass Mesa. The valley's population had grown slowly since 600, and in some periods had even declined. As a settlement pattern, dispersed communities of small hamlets prevailed. But beginning about 850, following a time when the population had dropped dramatically, new villages, including McPhee and Grass Mesa, emerged. By 860, the valley experienced a population explosion. Richard concluded that higher birth rates alone

**Crow Canyon archaeologist Richard Wilshusen examining a stratigraphic profile.** Photo courtesy of Richard Wilshusen.

could not have produced such growth. Instead, people were immigrating from some unknown area. By 865 to 870, when Richard believed the valley's population was greatest, he estimated that a total of some 2,860 men, women, and children were living there. Household residences (what Ricky Lightfoot called *architectural suites* at Duckfoot) were still distinguishable in the villages, but they formed multi-residential complexes averaging ten households each.

In comparing villages with dispersed settlements, Richard concluded that the "cost" of farming was higher for households in villages than it was for dispersed households. The primary reason was that dispersed settlers lived closer to their fields than did many villagers, who had to go greater distances to tend their crops. Villages, however, could exercise more control over the land. And in times of drought or short growing seasons, when food shortages struck, it was easier for village residents to share stored surpluses or small harvests than it was for families who were scattered across the landscape. The impact of the shortfall was averaged out among all villagers.

*When people returned...they built their new homes directly on top of, or immediately adjacent to, the houses that had been abandoned decades earlier. This is a common phenomenon at many of the ancient Pueblo Indian homesites scattered across the Four Corners country. I have often wondered why new homes were built on top of old ones rather than in some more pristine area nearby. As a land-use practice, it makes good sense. Why use good farmland as a new homesite when the old site would do? Some of the structures and building materials at the old sites might have been incorporated into new homes in the same spot.*

*Preserving farmland and using existing structures and materials are practical reasons for building new homes on top of old ones. But people are rarely that practical. In America today we are burying our best farmlands beneath sprawling suburbs while...abandoning perfectly sound buildings in our older cities. Were those ancient Puebloans more practical than we?*

*I asked a Pueblo Indian from Santa Clara, New Mexico, why his ancestors chose to build their new homes on top of older ones. His answer had nothing to do with practicality. Once a house is built and occupied, he said, it becomes a sacred place. His ancestors chose to build their new homes on sites that had already been made sacred by people living in them in earlier times. That is probably as close as I'll ever get to knowing why ancient Puebloan people here built their new homes on top of old ones.*

—Ian Thompson
**"Four Corners Almanac"**[3]

Richard reviewed 60 years of research into ninth-century sites throughout the Mesa Verde region and identified 30 sites, including eight in the Dolores Valley, that met his criteria for villages. In several cases he found the villages and remapped them. All of them, with the exception of Cirque Village, lay at the higher limits of the corn-growing elevations in the San Juan Basin. Most were relatively short-lived. Indeed, archaeologists are finding that the Dolores River Valley may have been abandoned and resettled several times between 600 and 900. Puebloan farmers were much more flexible and mobile before 900 than anyone previously supposed.

A study by Richard Wilshusen and archaeologist Sarah Schlanger looked at tree-ring information and identified four periods of drought between 600 and 910. The tree-ring data indicated that little or no construction or remodeling took place in settlements in the Dolores River Valley during the drought years. Sarah and Richard also looked at the way the Puebloans treated their buildings when they abandoned them at the onset of each drought. They concluded that the first three droughts prompted only short-distance moves. The abandoned structures were left relatively intact, and people took most objects in them along to their new homes.

The onset of the last ninth-century drought came in 880, when Richard estimated that 2,860 people lived in the valley. As people left this time, they deliberately burned many pit structures and left heavier items behind. Sarah and Richard interpreted this to mean that people moved some distance away and did not intend to return. And indeed, with a few minor, short-lived exceptions, the Dolores River Valley never again saw permanent residents until the arrival of white settlers in the late nineteenth century.

As people were leaving the Dolores River Valley at the end of the ninth century, what was happening elsewhere in the Mesa Verde region?

The spectacular cliff dwellings in Mesa Verde National Park attract hundreds of thousands of visitors from throughout the world every year. Built in the early 1200s, these stone villages sheltered Puebloan families for decades until the people departed the entire San Juan Basin forever at the end of that century. Visitors today are struck by the beauty of the buildings and their settings, and they try to imagine what life was like there centuries ago. But the strongest image usually is the one evoked by the sense of abandonment. Why would the Puebloans choose to leave their homes in such a beautiful natural setting?

Visitors frequently leave the park with the impression that it, along with the entire San Juan Basin, was continuously inhabited for many centuries by a peaceful agricultural people, who gradually progressed from living in pit structures to living in the enduring stone residences most visible today. Until recently, that was a point of view shared by most archaeologists too. Few Southwestern archaeologists recognized an earlier abandonment of the region that lasted for most of the tenth century. The abandonment of the Dolores River Valley was a part of it.

Mark Varien, director of research at the Crow Canyon Archaeological Center, plotted 3,301 tree-ring cutting dates from throughout the Mesa Verde region, beginning with the fifth century and ending near the end of the thirteenth. The plot showed a pronounced surge in cutting dates between 850 and 880, dates that correspond to the occupancy of Duckfoot, the villages in the Dolores Valley, and other heavily settled areas of the region. That peak was followed by a dramatic drop to almost no cutting dates for the entire tenth century. Then the number began to rise again in the early eleventh century.

Were any Pueblo Indians living in the Mesa Verde region in the 900s? Considering that there were a few cutting dates from that century, a few people probably lived there during that time. If so, then life for them could have borne little resemblance to the village life of their late-ninth-century forebearers. Compara-tively speaking, it must have been a lonely existence.

Recognition of the near desertion of the Mesa Verde region in the tenth century is brand new and not widespread among Southwestern archaeologists. For that reason, little research focuses on where people went from there at that time. The people of Duckfoot went somewhere at about the same time the people of the nearby Dolores Valley went somewhere. Richard Wilshusen's research showed that all of the villages in his 30-village study, for which the necessary information was available, were deserted by the early 900s at the latest. Where did people go? Richard Wilshusen and Sarah Schlanger believed that settlement patterns and tree-ring cutting dates pointed to a massive relocation from the Mesa Verde region to northern New Mexico between 880 and the early 900s.

The San Juan River, where it flows through what is now New Mexico, forms the boundary between the so-called Mesa Verde archaeological region in the north and the Chaco archaeological region in the south.[4] The Mesa Verde archaeological region occupies southwestern Colorado, southeastern Utah, and a narrow slice of New Mexico north of the river. The Chaco region occupies northwestern New Mexico south of the San Juan. It is possible to stand on the riverbank in Shiprock, New Mexico, in the Mesa Verde archaeological region, and throw a stone across the river into the Chaco archaeological region where the Chaco River runs west from its headwaters in the Continental Divide. There the Chacoan core, the series of massive, multistoried stone pueblos for which Chaco Canyon is famous, sits along the west-running stretch of the river before it turns north toward the San Juan, which it joins about halfway between the towns of Farmington and Shiprock.

During the tenth century—while, according to Mark Varien's evaluation of the tree-ring record, human settlement in the Mesa Verde region was almost nonexistent—the population of the Chaco region grew. Gwinn Vivian, an archaeologist at the University of Arizona and a leading expert on ancient Chaco, cites studies showing that during the 900s the number of sites in the Chacoan core doubled, and that they increased sixfold in the Chuska Valley, immediately adjacent to the Chaco River in the west. Gwinn does not suggest that this population increase came from a migration from the Mesa Verde region across the San Juan. But the population increase suggests, in its own right, that a migration from as far north as the Dolores River Valley could account, in part, for population growth in the Chaco region.

Methods of determining where the new population originated might include determining if late ninth- and early tenth-century pottery from the Mesa Verde region was carried across the San Juan at that time. Some archaeologists, familiar with village layouts in the Dolores Valley in the late 800s, casually suggest that the same patterns can be seen in the initial construction phases of Pueblo Bonito, the eventually massive pueblo for which Chaco Canyon is best known. The idea is that architectural styles might have been transported south into Chaco. But there is no formal research focused on this question.

Population growth and the emergence of scattered clusters of small houses characterized settlement patterns in the Chaco region during the 900s. Once these small clusters were established, many became the locations of "great houses," and some, of "great kivas." The construction of the great houses often included a distinct masonry style associated with Chacoan culture, which is found also at so-called "outliers," Chaco-style pueblos throughout the San Juan Basin, and beyond. In short, the tenth century was a time when, from the perspective of twentieth-century archaeologists, the material elements of Chacoan culture became more distinct and defined within the region proper. This perspective would have important implications for the interpretation of cultural trends in the Mesa Verde region in the eleventh and twelfth centuries.

A *kiva*, in contrast to a *great kiva*, is a circular, subterranean structure often found in association with household residences in the Mesa Verde region after the eleventh century. Mesa Verdean kivas evolved from the pit houses found in earlier sites, such as those at Duckfoot and at villages in the Dolores River Valley. Like earlier pit houses, Mesa Verdean kivas were located in front, or south, of a masonry room block, between the room block and the village midden. They may have been used for special ceremonial events within households, but were also an important part of the domestic living space in Mesa Verdean household architecture.

*There is widespread interest among archaeologists in the pre-European "roads" found throughout the Four Corners country beyond Chaco Canyon. These features, which appear as linear grooves in the landscape, often bordered on one side or both by berms, were targeted for study at Chaco Canyon in the early 1970s. Examination of aerial photographs and subsequent ground survey revealed a network of these features in, and radiating from, Chaco Canyon. Some of the features are miles long and could link widely separated Chacoan-era pueblos. These may indeed qualify as transportation links—that is, roads.*

*But there are two reasons why not all of these groove-and-berm features should be called roads. Primarily, many of them, at least in Montezuma County, appear to be only a few hundred feet long and to go nowhere—hardly "roads." Second, to call all of them roads is likely to obscure other interpretations of their intended function. Some of them might be elements in what the archaeologist Mike Marshall calls the "ritual landscape" surrounding a single pueblo or a tight cluster of pueblos.*

—Ian Thompson
"Four Corners Almanac"[5]

Great kivas, on the other hand, are large, circular, nonresidential structures, 50 feet or more across, that held scores of people at a time. The only real similarities great kivas share with household kivas are their circular floor plan and the fact that they often sat partially below ground. Great kivas were prevalent at times in the San Juan Basin before the 900s; at other times they seem to have passed temporarily out of fashion. The kivas found in pueblos in New Mexico and Arizona today function rather like the ancient great kivas, serving the community, not the household.

Tenth-century Chaco region "great houses" are just what their name implies. Amid clusters of small houses, which continued to include pit structures, great houses were larger, more solidly built in a distinctive masonry style, sometimes multistoried, and often built on a elevation higher than the surrounding landscape. They included distinctive, interior Chacoan kivas—not great kivas—enclosed by a rectangle of masonry. Great houses began appearing in the Chaco region in the late A.D. 800s and early 900s.

Gwinn Vivian and other Chacoan archaeologists studying the era make the important point that the clusters of small houses came first. Great houses were built in those pre-existing clusters at a later time, leading to what archaeologist Stephen Lekson calls the "little bump, big bump" phenomenon. Today the small sites form low rubble mounds or "little bumps," and the collapsed multi-story great house forms the "big bump." Frequently, but not always, great kivas were built in the same clusters as great houses. That association of a great house with a great kiva within a cluster of smaller houses came to define further a community in the Chaco region after about 950, a time when there was little or no settlement in the Mesa Verde region. That the clusters of small houses formed first, implies that the founders of those Chacoan communities recognized them from the beginning as communities, well before their residents began building great houses and great kivas.

The evolution and definition of Chacoan communities carried into the eleventh century as population growth persisted. The great houses grew larger until, in the Chacoan core and adjacent locales, they became the massive, multistoried structures such as Pueblo Bonito that are now preserved in Chaco Culture National Historical Park. During the eleventh century, the communities themselves grew larger. The Chacoans made technological advances in water control systems that allowed residents to direct runoff from snowmelt and summer rains onto fields of corn, beans, and squash. And the "roads" for which Chacoan culture is known today began to appear throughout the region.

By the beginning of the 1000s too, people began to filter back into the Mesa Verde region, north of the San Juan. No archaeological research focused on the source of these new immigrants, simply because most researchers assumed that the Mesa Verde region remained densely peopled throughout the 900s. Only recently have a few archaeologists recognized

Crow Canyon archaeologist Mark Varien, 1991. Mark currently serves as the Director of Research at the Crow Canyon Archaeological Center.
© Catherine Elson, 1991.

the great drop in population, perhaps even the total abandonment, of the Mesa Verde region during the tenth century. If few researchers asked where the Mesa Verdeans went at the end of the 800s, it was because no one knew they had gone anywhere. Similarly, no one knew to ask where the new residents were coming from at the beginning of the 1000s.

Chacoan-style potsherds dating to the 1000s and primarily from the Chuska Valley were found at a number of sites in the Mesa Verde region. Chacoan or Chuskan sherds were found as far north as benches overlooking the Dolores Valley. Several interpretations stem from these sherds and other Chacoan artifacts and styles. Among them is a hypothesis that the Chuskan pots were trade wares brought into the Mesa Verdean communities from south of the San Juan. A second hypothesis holds that the sherds are an indication of Chacoan priests colonizing or even conquering existing Mesa Verdean communities, bringing with them their pottery and other Chacoan stylistic attributes, from architecture and roads to community organization.

What became apparent in the 1990s was that the history of the ancient Mesa Verde region and its peoples will have to be rewritten in the light of Richard Wilshusen's, Sarah

Schlanger's, and Mark Varien's evidence of population movements in the ninth through eleventh centuries, including the near-abandonment of the region in the tenth century. A new terminology, and perhaps even a new language, will have to be developed for writing that new history. It is difficult to imagine a sparsely settled landscape being "colonized" by Chacoan priests or "conquered" by Chacoan troops. The Mesa Verde region was more likely "settled" by new immigrants. Who those people were will be the subject of future research being designed by the Crow Canyon Archaeological Center and other institutions working in the Southwest. Were they descendants of the people who had inhabited the communities of the Mesa Verde region before the tenth century? Or were they a new people entirely? Regardless of who the new settlers

**A ghostly, blanketed figure passes beneath Holly House at Hovenweep National Monument in this photo from the turn of the 19th century.** Photo courtesy of Colorado Historical Society (10028081).

were, it is now possible, as Mark Varien puts it, to think of community histories in the region as having begun, or at least begun anew, at the end of the tenth century.

It is nearing noon, and Richard and I look south from the divide between the two river basins through the gap between Mesa Verde and Sleeping Ute Mountain. Across the San Juan River we can see into the Chuska Valley and the Chaco archaeological region. The sun is high in the eastern sky on this August morning in 1997, and we take one more look at the lake glittering below us. The poet Alfred Castner King was right in 1907 when he referred to the people as having forever departed the Dolores River Valley. But the Pueblo Indian history of the San Juan River Basin as a whole would continue for another 400 years.

*By the beginning of the eleventh century, people were returning to the Great Sage Plain and living in small houses dispersed across the mesa tops. The population grew and began a slow process of coming together into larger villages on the mesa tops. Bt the twelfth century, some of these villages were quite large and included great houses, masonry-lined great kivas, and roads similar to those built decades earlier in the Chaco basin. The population began expanding down the mesas toward the San Juan River. By the mid-thirteenth century these mesa-top villages were deserted, and people were living on the canyon rims on the Great Sage Plain and in the cliff dwellings on Mesa Verde. Towers and enclosed plazas replaced the earlier Chacoan-style buildings, though some of the mesa-top structures may have continued to be used by people living in the nearby canyon rim villages. When the people left these canyon villages, they left the region and never returned.*

—Ian Thompson
"Four Corners Almanac"[6]

I bid Richard goodbye, and he drives away for Chaco Canyon and the seventieth annual Pecos Conference, an informal meeting of archaeologists that will get underway there that evening. His journey will take him through the gap, across the San Juan, and deep into the Chaco region. As for me, I tarry awhile at that spot, reluctant to leave the sweeping vistas and the sense that I am surrounded by the drama of communities on the move.

# Chapter five

# *Sand Canyon Pueblo and the Great Emigration*

It was dawn when I left my home and drove west across the Great Sage Plain toward Sand Canyon Pueblo, a thirteenth-century walled village. Driving along gravel roads through vast, rolling fields and past well-kept farmhouses, I passed the sage-covered stone ruins of ancient Pueblo dwellings. I parked my pickup where the road crossed a small wooded hollow and walked to the head of a canyon, one of many that cut through the plain creating a series of narrow mesas. Ten miles away, the north escarpment of Mesa Verde rose 2,000 feet into the sky.

The ruins of Sand Canyon Pueblo, built around a spring and enclosed by a stone wall two and one-half feet thick, spread out before me. The wall held a vast complex of 420 rooms; 90 kivas; 14 stone towers two or three stories high whose function is debated; a great kiva 47 feet across where community-wide events may have been held; and adjacent to a plaza, a large D-shaped structure enclosing two kivas and several rooms.

Sand Canyon Pueblo and the Mesa Verde cliff dwellings were built just decades before the region was abandoned around 1300. Until recently, scholars assumed the exodus was caused by a severe drought between 1276 and 1300. Researchers at the Crow Canyon Archaeological Center are investigating whether depletion of forests and game, and even warfare, might have played

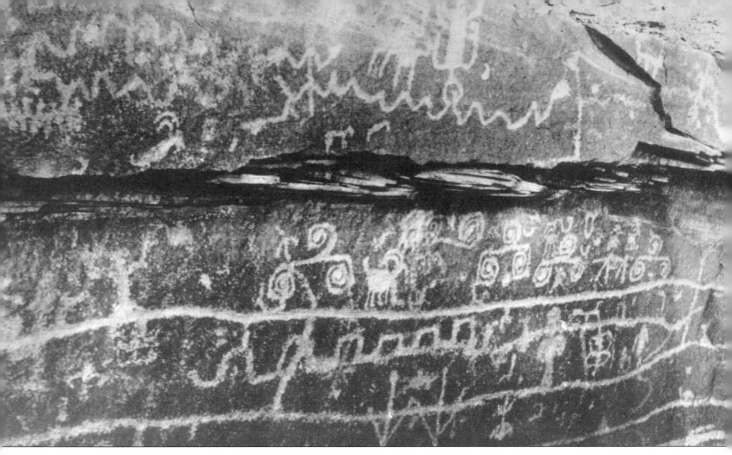

**Petroglyph panel (ca. 1913) in Yellowjacket Canyon.** Photo courtesy of Colorado Historical Society (10028078).

a role. The Sand Canyon Project is also studying the formation and development of Puebloan communities in the Mesa Verde region.

When Crow Canyon's E. Charles Adams and Bruce Bradley first mapped Sand Canyon Pueblo in the early 1980s, they noticed that the buildings were grouped into 15 separate units consisting of kivas and contiguous blocks of rooms. Bradley referred to each kiva and its adjacent rooms as a *kiva suite*. Adams and Bradley found the ratio of rooms to kivas (420:90) at Sand Canyon to be much lower than at contemporaneous Mesa Verde pueblos such as Cliff Palace (217:23) and Spruce Tree House (114:8). Because kivas were thought to be places for religious ceremonies, similar to those in modern-day pueblos, they reasoned that Sand Canyon Pueblo might have been a ceremonial center.

Bradley, James Kleidon, and Melissa Churchill spent ten years excavating 12 percent of the site's structures, including kivas, rooms, parts of the great kiva, the D-shaped structure, and the wall. From tree-ring samples recovered from roof beams and other wood, they dated construction of the bulk of the pueblo to the 1240s, 1250s, and 1260s. The latest single date, 1277, indicates that the pueblo was at least partially inhabited until the final migrations from the area. Tree-ring dates varied within each architectural block, and unbonded masonry at wall abutments showed that some rooms were added to those already in place, leading Bradley to

*Sand Canyon Pueblo is a place that often inspires use of the word center in describing it—"ritual center," "trade center." The word creeps into the language of archaeologists and nonarchaeologists alike when they are speculating about the massive masonry complex dating to the thirteenth century.*

*The pueblo, contained within a crescent-shaped stone wall a third of a mile long, surrounds a forested canyon head high in a fertile plateau now planted in fields of wheat, beans, and alfalfa. From nearby ridges, the spot does seem centered in a vast circle of earth and sky bordered by distant mountains in Colorado, Utah, New Mexico, and Arizona. The word center, however, when applied to the pueblo, refers not to the natural landscape but to the thirteenth-century human landscape.*

—Ian Thompson
"Four Corners Almanac"[1]

conclude that each suite was built in several stages. He also discovered that a single kind of mortar was used in the great kiva, the D-shaped structure, and the enclosing wall, suggesting that these structures were built at the same time. The mortar used in the kiva suites was different, indicating separate construction. The way in which kiva suites abutted the perimeter wall suggested that they were built later. Bradley theorized that the entire pueblo, though built over three or four decades, was planned in advance. The amount of organized labor required for such a large project indicated a high degree of community organization.

If the pueblo were a ceremonial center, then what about the surrounding settlements it might have served? Crow Canyon archaeologist William Lipe framed a series of questions that guided the search for answers: Why did settlement patterns in the region change from widely dispersed farms to concentrations of people in large villages? What was the economic and social organization within settlements? Were environmental changes, such as severe drought or resource depletion, responsible for the final exodus? He then proposed a survey of the area around Sand Canyon and nearby Goodman Point pueblos. Between 1985 and 1987, Carla Van West and Michael Adler directed teams that mapped and recorded 429 sites in a 10-square-mile area. Each site was assigned a general time period based on styles of pottery and architecture visible on the surface. They concluded that the area was inhabited, with occasional periods of abandonment, for some 700 years, from about 600 to 1300.

**An excavated roomblock and kiva at Sand Canyon Pueblo.** © Crow Canyon Archaeological Center, 1988.

Adler, then a doctoral candidate at the University of Michigan, looked for ways to recognize communities in the archaeological record. He found that in 28 similar modern farming cultures in Africa and elsewhere, settlements were often centered on large public structures where community events were held. In mapping the area around Sand Canyon and Goodman Point, he discovered two distinct clusters of sites separated by a mile-wide expanse of mesa top. Adler suggested that these clusters might represent communities. A third community seems to have encompassed Castle Rock, another pueblo six miles south of Sand Canyon.

Pottery and architectural styles indicated that these site clusters began forming in the late tenth or early eleventh century. Initially, each one consisted of widely dispersed structures, five to ten rooms and one or two kivas in each, accommodating one or two families. Over time, somewhat larger residential buildings appeared, with more rooms and more kivas, serving as home for more families living side-by-side. By the early twelfth century, each cluster of sites had a great kiva large enough to hold community-wide events. Eventually, Sand Canyon and Goodman Point pueblos, the final architectural additions to the survey area, were built near the center of each cluster.

Changes in pottery and architectural styles suggested that community-wide moves from mesa-top sites to nearby canyon residences took place in the early to middle thirteenth century. Between 1988 and 1991, Crow Canyon's Mark Varien and Kristin Kuckelman excavated six sites on the mesa top and four on or just below the canyon rim. At mesa-top sites they found no large roof beams for tree-ring dating. The beams had probably been salvaged for use in constructing new buildings nearby, a practice common in many historic pueblos. There were also few artifacts on the floors of rooms, suggesting that the people took pottery vessels and other household equipment to their new homes. Small pieces of charcoal were unearthed and analyzed for tree-ring dates. These and pottery dates showed that all but one of the mesa-top sites was abandoned by roughly 1240, probably about the time that construction of Sand Canyon Pueblo began.

Dates from four sites on or just below the canyon rims indicated that they were built later than those on the mesa tops and inhabited into the mid-1200s. This confirmed the theory that a move from residences on the mesa tops to ones in the canyons took place

*If there is a spring within an ancient pueblo, it is usually in a shaded overhang beneath the cliff.... When I go to the canyon-rim pueblos on the Great Sage Plain with living Pueblo Indians from New Mexico and Arizona, they inevitably speak of the significance of the spring—not just for the people who once lived there but also for today's Pueblo Indians when they return there. On hot summer days it is easy to comprehend the very real importance of the spring to the people who once lived in those pueblos. The spring is often the only source of water for miles around. Not only would it have provided drinking and cooking water, but the spring would have been a source of water to nurture plants in nearby gardens. It is possible, too, to begin comprehending the symbolic importance of these springs to living Pueblo Indians. Springs and lakes are woven into the emergence traditions of all modern pueblos. They are seen not merely as a source of water but as the source of all life.*

—Ian Thompson
"Four Corners Almanac"[2]

in the first half of the thirteenth century. By mid-century, people were moving into the walled pueblo itself, perhaps to defend against hostile neighbors or to be near the spring. Excavation of kivas and middens in the pueblo revealed copious amounts of domestic artifacts and refuse, leading Bradley to reject the initial hypothesis that the place was strictly a nonresidential ceremonial center.

Studies of animal remains are also beginning to shed light on Sand Canyon's community organization. Jonathan Driver, a faunal expert from Simon Fraser University, studied the animal bones found at all of the excavated sites in the study area. At earlier mesa-top sites, the proportion of deer bone hovered consistently near 5 percent. In the small, thirteenth-century, canyon-rim sites contemporaneous with the pueblo, deer bone was virtually absent, but in the pueblo itself a striking 14 percent of the bones were from deer. Driver suggested that deer might have been a favored food and that its abundance at the pueblo and near-absence from smaller canyon-rim sites could indicate either that deer hunting was controlled from within the pueblo or that deer carcasses were regularly taken there for community feasts.

Crow Canyon's Chris Pierce directed pottery studies aimed at understanding the degree to which the different communities interacted. In one study, he looked for evidence of pottery manufacture—including polishing stones, unfired pots, and unused raw clay—at excavated sites in the Sand Canyon and Castle Rock communities. All three kinds of artifacts were found at some sites but not others, suggesting that pottery might have been produced only in certain locations and then traded or exchanged within the communities.

Another study designed by Pierce and conducted by research associate Maggie Thurs looked at the crushed igneous rock used for temper in Mesa Verde Black-on-white bowls, common throughout the region between about 1180 and 1300. The nearest source of igneous rock lies in the Castle Rock community. Not surprisingly, 20 percent of the bowls from Castle Rock Pueblo contained igneous temper, compared with only 4 percent of those from Sand Canyon Pueblo. What was surprising was that 47 percent and 50 percent, respectively, of bowls from two of the tested canyon-rim sites well within Sand Canyon were made with igneous temper. In a third study, research associate Donna Glowacki, a graduate student at the University of Missouri, used *neutron activation analysis* to tie pots to particular clay sources by their chemical composition. Some bowls from Sand Canyon Pueblo were made of clay from Mesa Verde and Castle Rock—both well outside the Sand Canyon community.

Adler defined communities by looking at the density of sites in the survey area. He drew boundaries where the number of sites fell off dramatically. The pottery studies indicated that proximity alone did not dictate distribution and exchange. The peoples' social and economic life was more complex than settlement patterns alone suggest.

Another factor that probably affected interactions among communities was the rugged terrain. As part of his doctoral research at Arizona State University, Mark Varien explored the role the deep canyons played in shaping the boundaries of local communities. Walking time influences how far people are willing to go to plant crops or gather wood, and Varien used new computer programs to calculate walking time across varying terrain.

Traditionally, explanations of the exodus from the Mesa Verde region focused on drought. Carla Van West studied the effect of drought on the agricultural productivity of the Great Sage Plain. Using ethnographic examples from historical pueblos and Mexican peasant communities to calculate the amount of corn needed to feed populations of various sizes, she demonstrated that the drought would not have diminished corn production to the point of forcing all the people to emigrate.

**Mesa Verde Black-on-white kiva jar (ca. A.D. 1270), found on the floor of a masonry tower at Castle Rock Pueblo during Crow Canyon's excavations, 1990–1994.** © Crow Canyon Archaeological Center, 1994.

Some archaeologists suggest that deforestation and the exhaustion of construction timber and firewood might have played a role in the abandonment. As part of his master's thesis research at Northern Arizona University, Mark Hovezak studied the effects of the construction of Sand Canyon Pueblo on the surrounding forest. The pueblo's kivas would have required more than 13,500 beams, and many more went into the 420 rooms and 14 towers. Using data on tree growth rates in nearby areas deforested in modern times, Hovezak concluded that harvesting construction timber around the pueblo would not have caused complete deforestation. Archaeological evidence supports this conclusion: a common indicator of deforestation is the presence of less desirable fuels, such as desert bushes, in hearths, and no such evidence was found anywhere in the Sand Canyon community.

Whatever forced them to leave, there was a dark side to those final days. At Castle Rock Pueblo, Crow Canyon archaeologists Kristin Kuckelman and Ricky Lightfoot found evidence of violent conflict dating to the end of occupation in about 1280. All or parts of 41 skeletons, none of which appeared to have been formally buried, lay scattered throughout the site. Analysis of two skulls revealed evidence of fatal blows to the head.

Lightfoot and Kuckelman concluded that either all of Castle Rock's last residents were killed in battle or, if there were survivors, they fled quickly, leaving their dead unburied.

More than 50 thirteenth-century pueblos similar to Sand Canyon and Goodman Point dot the Great Sage Plain, all waiting to be studied. Crow Canyon research directors Richard Wilshusen and, later, Mark Varien formulated new sets of questions that will join Lipe's list in guiding research in the years ahead. Like Lipe's, these questions concern community organization and the role of environment in shaping communities, but they focus more on the economic and cultural relationships among the communities of the Mesa Verde region.

One burning question remains: Why was emigration from the region so complete? The answer will be sought on the Great Sage Plain and where the people of the Mesa Verde region went: the Rio Grande Valley in New Mexico; the Little Colorado River Valley in Arizona; and perhaps to scattered locations even farther south. The closest are only a few days' walk away; the farthest, a couple of weeks.[3]

# Chapter six

## *Messages on the Landscape*

*I drove through vast bean fields with friends recently on our way to the great expanses of sage that stretch from the last fields to the bluffs overlooking the San Juan River. We were searching for traces of agriculture. On one gentle slope we saw native plants aligned in long parallel rows. They could be rooted in centuries-old rock farming terraces now covered by windblown soil. The vegetation alignments were first spotted by aerial archaeologists Tom and Lee Baker of Albuquerque. They sent me photographs, and I searched out the features on foot. Looking at the alignments on the ground, it is impossible to tell whether they are ancient or modern. Only through careful archaeological testing could that be determined....*

*Scattered through the expanses of sage are exposed patches of gently sloping slickrock. Today they are frequently the locations of modern stock ponds that collect water running off the rock during storms. The modern dams are built atop or near ancient dams that served the same purpose.... It is easy to imagine the collected water being carried from the reservoirs to nearby garden plots centuries ago.*

*The puzzling thing about the Puebloan agriculture that was practiced here for more than a thousand years is that it left so little trace on the landscape. The people's houses can be found and their "roads" are still evident, but those ancient Puebloan fields have vanished.*

—Ian Thompson
"Four Corners Almanac"[1]

**Editor's note:** This chapter was previously published in a slightly different form in a collection of papers on Puebloan architecture. Sandy Thompson was the senior author, with Mark Varien, Susan Kenzle, and Rina Swentzell as coauthors.

The architecture of thirteenth-century Puebloan hamlets and villages in southwestern Colorado and southeastern Utah is dominated by residential room blocks, kivas, and towers. Because archaeologists are most often concerned with matters such as site population, function, use-life, and dating, they tend to focus on readily apparent features.

Yet the Puebloan world of the thirteenth-century hamlets and villages was also characterized by more subtle forms of architecture. Low stone walls, for instance, connect and enclose structures that in turn create enclosed interior plazas. Stone circles and rectangles appear in the landscape. Stone alignments that are not walls surround parts or all of certain pueblos and sometimes contain boulders weighing a ton or more. Site reports occasionally mention these features in passing, but may refer to them as terraces, retaining walls, water control devices, or defensive features. In some cases, they might not have served any of these functions.

At the Crow Canyon Archaeological Center, such subtle forms of architecture are called *Architecture With Unknown Function* (AWUF). From the perspective of archaeological research, such features may help us better understand human interaction within and between communities. From the perspective of Puebloan cosmology, they may help to place built communities in the larger natural and spiritual world.

A first encounter with AWUF is often surprising, because it forces one to recognize that the boundaries of an archaeological site can merge into the landscape beyond the well-defined rubble of rooms, kivas, towers, and middens. That recognition came when Mark Varien and I stood on a low, eroded bench overlooking the Rio Puerco, surrounded by a vast and brilliant sweep of northeastern Arizona. With us were archaeologists John Stein and Andrew Fowler. It was our first visit there; for Stein and Fowler, it was one more weekend pursuing a project to which they gave thousands of hours of their own time. What we saw at the remains of a twelfth-century pueblo was a distinct mound of masonry rubble that was once a tall public structure, or "great house," with associated blocks of rooms set in a place of arroyos and eroded red earth.

Stein and Fowler proceeded to expand our initial perception of the site by pointing out more subtle architectural features reaching into the surrounding landscape. They began with a series of low, curving, subtle earthen berms, or walls, nearly encircling the rubble mounds and adjacent areas. From one opening in the encircling berm, another long, linear berm and swale, which they called a road, extended east several hundred meters and pointed toward another great house that lay beyond the horizon. Other such features radiated out in various directions from the great house. Suddenly an archaeological site that we viewed only moments before as covering a few hundred square meters stretched over thousands of square meters, encompassing much more than the obvious rubble mound.

We returned home wondering whether similar features might be associated with archaeological sites in southwestern Colorado. We began by looking at large, thirteenth-century pueblos. Indeed, they included architecture extending beyond room blocks, kivas, and towers—though these features were made of stone rather than earth. Casual surveys in southeastern Utah supported the preliminary conclusion that stone AWUF existed at some late sites in the Mesa Verde region.

At about the time that stone AWUF began to appear, there were other changes in the Puebloan world. People were coming together from small hamlets scattered across fertile mesa tops into larger villages, some of which were newly located in the rockier environment of canyon rims, slopes, and bottoms.

We can place AWUF in an archaeological setting by looking briefly at settlement patterns in the Mesa Verde region—that is, at the distribution of sites across the landscape.

From 900 to 1300, during the *Pueblo II* (900–1150) and *Pueblo III* (1150–1300) periods, many changes occurred. If we focus on buildings and sites, some of the important changes include an increase in site size, greater use of stone masonry, an increase in the diversity of site layouts, and a change in site location. If we expand our field of vision and focus on the region, we see another important change: a dramatic shift in the way communities were organized. These changes in community organization are a key to explaining the changes in buildings and sites.

Around 900, at the beginning of the Pueblo II period, the archaeological landscape was dotted with small, remarkably similar habitation units. Most consisted of a group of contiguous surface rooms, a subterranean kiva, and a midden containing discarded artifacts, ashy sediments, and human burials. The buildings on sites of the early Pueblo II period were usually made from earth and timber, but not masonry. The layout of these sites is so remarkably standard that T. Mitchell Prudden, a researcher at the turn of the twentieth century, labeled them "unit pueblos," and archaeologists continue to call them unit pueblos or Prudden units.

At first glance, these small sites might appear to be evenly scattered across the landscape. Archaeologist Michael Adler surveyed Sand Canyon and found that settlements were not evenly dispersed. Instead, clusters of numerous small sites were separated by areas with relatively few sites. We believe these clusters of small sites represent communities.

By the late Pueblo II period, many of these dispersed communities included some type of public architecture, usually a great kiva or a great house, which was the location of community rituals that helped integrate the surrounding small habitation sites. We call these buildings "public architecture" because of their size, the details of their construction, and the fact that they appear less frequently than habitation sites. The great kivas are too large to have been used by just a few families, and the great houses are constructed with different techniques and materials that make them seem monumental when compared with habitation sites.

As Pueblo II gave way to Pueblo III, between 1100 and 1150, two interesting things happened. First, the small sites became bigger. Instead of one or two kivas, there were three, four, or more. Second, individual unit pueblos were located closer together. This process resulted in clusters of small sites so closely spaced that archaeologists consider them a single aggregated site. Some of these became large enough to be villages. Aggregated sites became most common in the 1200s, when we see the peak of population density in the Mesa Verde region and first begin to notice AWUF.

What exactly does Architecture With Unknown Function consist of?

First, there are *low stone walls*. They appear at sites of varying sizes, usually situated on canyon rims and around canyon heads. Sites at such locations generally stretch along the top of the cliff and spill down onto the talus slope below. The low stone walls are constructed of rough-hewn, rectangular, sandstone blocks, and enclose the architecture at the top of

**A remote, well-preserved site on Cedar Mesa.** © Ricky Lightfoot.

the cliff. In a few cases the wall may be traced across the talus below, but frequently either erosion erased it from the talus or it was never there at all. At cliff-edge and canyon-head sites, low stone walls sometimes connect room blocks, towers, and public architecture. At many of these sites the low stone enclosing wall juts out in some places to form a semicircular arc, never more than two meters across, and then resumes its linear run.

Preservation of these walls varies from one site to the next and within sites. Some sites include short segments of fully standing perimeter walls, and from these intact remnants one can draw inferences about the general appearance and construction of low walls at other sites. Judging from research done in the Mesa Verde region, it appears that the perimeter walls were similar from site to site. This leads, in turn, to the inference that they served a similar function everywhere.

The majority of the perimeter walls in the Mesa Verde region were relatively low; most of them stood between half a meter high and one and a half meters high. In addition, most of the fully enclosing perimeter walls had openings, or gates, that allowed entry from outside and offered access into public areas such as plazas. In effect, it appears that these walls served to channel visitors into public areas where the residents could see them. Archaeologist Stephen Lekson reached a similar conclusion about the long, low walls found at sites in Chaco Canyon.

The relatively sudden and widespread appearance of low stone walls at sites built during the Pueblo III period is important to our understanding of social relationships in the final decades preceding abandonment of the Mesa Verde region. It is possible that these low walls served social convention and functioned like the fences around houses today. They probably served more than one purpose. According to architectural historian Paul Oliver, in some cultures perimeter walls define a community's boundaries and function as mundane physical embodiments of cosmological boundaries.

Access between cliff-top and talus structures was frequently gained through *enclosed cracks* in the cliff that were wide enough to allow human passage. The tops of these cracks were often enclosed by towers or low, circular stone walls.

In addition to true walls, we also found *aligned stones*. These are not walls, but unworked stones and boulders aligned to enclose part or all of a site. They are present in at least three canyon-bottom sites built in association with buttes or natural monoliths. In some cases the boulders weigh a ton or more. At two sites built adjacent to and atop buttes in southeastern Utah, the stone alignments run along the edge of the caprock on top of the butte and around structures at its base. At Castle Rock Pueblo, a canyon-bottom site where Crow Canyon Archaeological Center conducted test excavations, the aligned stones completely enclose structures at the south base of a natural monolith. However, except for a few short segments, they do not enclose the structures at the north base of the monolith.

Sandy Thompson (center) with Tito Naranjo (Santa Clara Pueblo) and Esther Martinez (San Juan Pueblo) at Woods Canyon Pueblo in 1994, discussing the meaning and importance of AWUF. © Crow Canyon Archaeological Center, 1994.

We also identified *large stone circles*. These are circles formed of unworked stone, usually measuring 4 to 5 meters in diameter. Some such circles lie within the perimeters of sites, but they occur in isolation, too, at some distance from residential sites.

Finally, we found *small stone rectangles*. These lie immediately outside a site's perimeter and usually measure about a meter across and one and one-half meters long. Such rectangles appeared at several sites; three of them were clustered just outside Castle Rock Pueblo.

Pueblo people, who live today in communities with histories and architectural traditions rooted deep in the past, may find the kinds of architectural expression that is noted here more familiar than archaeologists or western-trained architects do. One such person is Rina Swentzell, an architectural historian, educator, and member of the Santa Clara Pueblo.

Here are Rina's thoughts on the meaning and importance of AWUF:

> These "constructions" went unnoticed by earlier archaeologists because Puebloan "architecture" is defined not by Puebloans but by Western people who look for what they define as architecture. Puebloans do not view their own architecture the way it is viewed by Western people.
>
> In the Western world, architecture is altogether contained within the human landscape: it considers only the human context. Indeed, Western architecture is about human genius and ego. It does not often consider any larger contexts—particularly the natural context. Architecture in the Western world is really about human constructions, and great attention is paid to the types of construction materials used and the manipulation of those materials. It focuses on the walls, or that which defines space, rather than on the contained space. It is very material-oriented.
>
> "Architecture" is a misnomer when applied to Puebloan constructions over the last 1,500 years because the word does not capture the full scope of space definitions or the symbolic nature of Puebloan building. For the Pueblo people, the human landscape is meaningless outside the natural context; human constructions are not considered separately from their relationship to the hills, valleys, and mountains. Buildings and structures, and their walls, are not the primary focus. They are extensions of the natural world and, therefore, do not call attention to themselves or their makers. They are meaningful only as containers—for the function served by the described spaces and for the cosmic relationships that they reiterate.

At a site in Montezuma County, for example, one naturally paved plaza has direct reference to the canyon space below. A smaller naturally paved area, bounded by house structures and low walls, leads into the plaza space, which then opens and drops into the canyon. The focus of the plaza space on the canyon space acknowledges the larger feminine space of the canyon, while also establishing a visual relationship with another pueblo across the canyon, a peak in the distance, and the sky beyond.

Puebloan constructions are significant parts of a highly symbolic world. Bears, rainbows, and rain can be pulled out of walls. Lakes are contained within houses and kivas. In this world, human beings live on a daily and intimate basis with the movement in the sky and acknowledgment of simultaneous existences in the underworld. Human existence is not contained within the material form of the human village; the human village is but one of the places where people make contact with movement in the sky and the underworld existences. Many other such places—spaces—described by hills, concavities, rock outcroppings, naturally paved areas, and human-built walls extend throughout this defined "world."

Even today, that defined "world" is bounded by the far mountains and includes hills, valleys, lakes, and springs. These natural boundaries define the space within which the people live. Points or places within the natural environment that connect with the region beyond, or with worlds below, or the sky above are often marked by a single stone, piles of stone, circles of stone, stones placed on end, or concavities in the ground or bedrock. Often, human constructions are a part of natural formations such as cliffs, stone outcroppings, or natural concavities.

In several thirteenth-century sites in Montezuma County, there are circular areas defined by loose alignments of stones. These areas are similar to those found around modern pueblos; they are where the living people meet the cloud beings. These are places visited by the people of this fourth world to make connections with the breath of the cosmos, with the underworld, and with the cloud people/spirits, the deer/buffalo people/spirits, or the water serpent.

The entire "world" is intimately known, acknowledged, and used. Spatial use and organization are not limited to the village area. The material village is one of the concentric rings about the symbolic center of the world. It is not given more weight or focus than the area of the fields, hills, or mountains. It constitutes one place within the whole. The web of human existence is interlaced with what happens in the larger natural context and therefore flows into the adjacent spaces, hills, and mountains. All constructions within that context, including AWUF, acknowledge the intertwining life forces within which human existence happens.

*Rina Swentzell looks at sites from a perspective markedly different from my own. Once, while visiting sites where archaeologists and astronomers suspect that buildings were aligned with the sun's rays on the summer solstice, I remembered a trip Rina and I made to "Puzzle House," a site then being excavated by Jim Judge and his students at Fort Lewis College in Durango. Rina was as puzzled as anyone else by what emerged as excavation progressed. Later, as we explored other sites nearby, she cautioned me not to get too carried away looking for relationships between architecture and astronomical bodies and events. Puebloan architecture in general, she feels, is oriented more to the earth than to the sky. Ancient astronomical markers would have been so subtle that they are probably no longer visible on the landscape, or they might have been petroglyphs related to a nearby natural feature.*

*The summer solstice is a significant event in many modern pueblos, and it probably was in ancient pueblos as well. As a result of my day with Rina, I won't be disappointed if I find no relationship between major structures and the place where the summer solstice sun rose. I'll turn my attention to looking for something more subtle in the nearby landscape.*

—Ian Thompson
"Four Corners Almanac"[2]

When contrasted with the residential and large public structures at archaeological sites, the most significant characteristic of AWUF is its subtlety. It is easily overlooked in studying and interpreting sites. Indeed, according to some accounts, a substantial amount of AWUF was hauled away from Aztec National Monument in northwestern New Mexico and used for roadfill, thus ensuring that the pueblo will never be fully understood.

We are a long way from comprehending the functions of AWUF; thus, the name stands. We can safely say, however, that it offers the promise of a better understanding of human movement toward and within communities, and of the place of the human community in the natural world.[3]

**Aerial view of the Great Sage Plain and the Sleeping Ute Mountain, one of the Four Corners' landmark features.**
© Walter BigBee, *Comanche*, 2001.

✳

## Chapter seven

# Histories Well-Told; Secrets Well-Kept

My home, an hour's drive west of Sunnyside Mesa, commands a spectacular view of Sleeping Ute Mountain on the Ute Mountain Ute Reservation a few miles southwest. Directly south is Mesa Verde, where Mesa Verde National Park with its spectacular Puebloan cliff dwellings, is located. From a north window I can look north and northwest across the Great Sage Plain, which contains tens of thousands of archaeological sites representing several centuries of Puebloan history before the final migration from the area in the late 1200s. The Puebloans who lived here are among the ancestors of the modern Puebloan peoples who live today in New Mexico and Arizona. Each of those communities preserves its migration stories in oral traditions.

No one knows how many Puebloan archaeological sites exist in the San Juan Basin. Only a small percentage of them, say 10,000 to 15,000, lie within the boundaries of national parks and monuments including Mesa Verde, Chaco Canyon, Aztec, Hovenweep, Navajo, and Canyon de Chelly. The interpretation of publicly accessible sites in these parks and monuments is carried out almost exclusively from the archaeologists' point of view. That interpretation is based on a description of changes in material culture—architecture and artifacts— in a chronological sequence usually spanning the time between when corn was first grown here and the final Puebloan migrations from the region. The

connection between these sites and the modern Pueblo communities not far outside the basin is made only in passing. Pueblo Indians frequently criticize these interpretations for omitting or downplaying the continuity that exists between places such as Cliff Palace or Pueblo Bonito and modern Puebloan communities.

In 1992, I began a project for the Four Corners Heritage Council that was designed to invite Pueblo Indians to offer their interpretations of archaeological sites and prominent landforms that are managed for public visitation. Following the advice of American Indian members of the Heritage Council, I observed protocol by sending a written description of the project to appropriate tribal leaders, and by making appointments to travel to several communities to discuss it. I also met with leaders of American Indian organizations including the All Indian Pueblo Council.

I began with the Hopi and traveled east toward the Rio Grande. No one I spoke with openly opposed the concept, but no one eagerly embraced it, either. I was not prepared for this. I had expected the Pueblo communities to be eager to participate in the public interpretation of their own past.

The reasons I was given for this cool reception were the same in each community. First, maintaining confidentiality is a requirement applied to specific elements of oral tradition. Sharing certain knowledge decreases its effectiveness in maintaining Puebloan cultures and communities as a whole. Some knowledge cannot even be shared among groups within a particular community, much less with the non-Indian public.

Second, I had proposed not only to involve living Pueblo Indians in introducing their perspectives into interpretations of sites and landforms, but also to use written migration accounts found in the existing ethnographic literature, including that written by American Indian anthropologists themselves. This goal was strongly criticized because people almost universally felt that those written accounts were inappropriately obtained, inappropriately presented, and frequently inaccurate.

Third, there was a strong feeling that non-Indians obtained traditional community knowledge for their own personal enrichment—to sell books on the subject—and that no benefits from sharing this knowledge ever made their way back to the communities themselves.

Finally, American Indians who do share traditional knowledge with non-Indians without consulting the appropriate elders are subjected to ostracism within their communities. I spoke with several American Indians who are employed as interpreters for the National Park Service. They are often severely criticized at home for their work.

I was told the project might work if it were controlled, designed, and executed by American Indians themselves. The project was eventually redesigned by a committee composed entirely of American Indians, with sponsorship and support from—but no control by—the Four Corners Heritage Council. The concept evolved and bore little resemblance to my original proposal. A demonstration project would be conducted in the Ute Mountain Tribal Park on the Ute Mountain Ute Reservation. The tribal park adjoins Mesa Verde National Park on the south and includes both Puebloan and Ute ancestral sites. Visitors would be accompanied by Ute interpreters and guides. One important element of that new interpretation would be to explain to non-Indian visitors why confidentiality or secrecy is so important to the continued survival of American Indian cultures and communities.

As each modern Pueblo community maintains oral accounts of the migration from this area to where they are today, so too, my family's oral history tells of our migration. After my mother's great-grandfather settled with his eight sons near Boulder in 1860, some of his descendants migrated

**Southern Ute man with infant, ca. 1915.**
Photo courtesy of La Plata County Historical Society.

over the next half-century, stopping along the way, to extreme southwestern Colorado, where they are today. My mother told me most of what I know about this migration.

There are a few written records of my family's Colorado past. They include a family "history" containing birth, marriage, and death dates and places and little more—a sort of geographical genealogy. There is an essay by my great-grandmother about the pastoral, apparently idyllic, life the family led at Oak Dell, their ranch in the Arkansas Valley. There are a few family letters. There are mentions of family members in local historical society publications in counties stretching from Boulder to La Plata counties. None of these written sources provides anything but a fragmented record of the movement of these people from northeast to southwest across Colorado. What I know of my family's migration story is drawn from my mother's oral accounts.

According to my mother, my great-great-grandfather Elija Eggleston, his eight sons, and their cattle arrived from Iowa and settled on South Boulder Creek, 25 miles north of

Denver, in 1860, in the wake of the gold rush of 1859. They came not to prospect for gold, but to produce food for the hordes of prospectors already there. They were Quakers, pacifists, and abolitionists. With the outbreak of the Civil War, my great-grandfather Wellington Kinsey Eggleston's abolitionist tendencies overcame his pacifist tendencies

**A Sunnyside Mesa homesteader with twins, ca. 1915.** Photo courtesy of La Plata County Historical Society.

and he returned to Iowa to join an Iowa regiment in the Union army. He returned to Colorado after the war with an Iowa bride, Ruth. By 1870, he established his own ranch, Oak Dell, near Salida, 110 miles southwest of Boulder. He completed dental school and opened an office in Salida in 1873. My grandmother, Myra Eggleston, one of 12 siblings, was born at Oak Dell in 1876.

By the mid-1880s, the ranch had been turned over to grown sons, and the remaining Eggleston family, including my grandmother, moved to the mining boomtown of Ouray, 95 miles southwest of Salida. There my great-grandfather opened a dentist's office and rode horse-back into the remote mining camps in the surrounding San Juans to practice dentistry. My grandmother attended Colorado A&M College, now Colorado

*The sunlit cliff dwelling looked out into the head of a narrow canyon shaded by tall Gambel oak and towering Douglas fir. Noisy jays, now gathering into autumn flocks, flew south beneath scattered clouds. We were in the Ute Mountain Tribal Park with Ute guide Ricky Hayes. He explained that the dwellings had been built in two stages before being abandoned in the early thirteenth century—in contrast to Cliff Palace, Spruce Tree House, and Balcony House in nearby Mesa Verde National Park, which were abandoned decades later....*

*Hayes based his interpretation of the cliff dwelling almost entirely upon scientific research findings. This was in part because the staff of the tribal park is reluctant to interpret the ancient dwellings from an American Indian perspective. The Utes are not descended from the Puebloans who once occupied the San Juan River Basin and feel that such interpretations should come only from Pueblo Indians.*

—Ian Thompson
"Four Corners Almanac"[1]

State University, in Fort Collins, where she studied botany. Following graduation she returned to Ouray and opened a greenhouse heated by a local hot spring. In 1906, she married my grandfather, John Nelson, a Swedish immigrant and a miner. My mother, one of three siblings, was born in Ouray in 1910.

In 1911, John Nelson traveled to Durango, 75 miles south-southwest of Ouray, in search of farmland. He filed on an abandoned homestead on Sunnyside Mesa, 15 miles south of Durango, and the family, including my mother, moved there in late 1911.

I end the story—which, to the best of my ability, I've told in my mother's words—at Sunnyside Mesa because, though none of my immediate family lives there now, it is in a sense my family's "center place." The house my grandfather built still stands and is occupied, my grandparents are buried there, and two cousins of my generation ranch and farm on Sunnyside Mesa. Nelson family reunions are still held there. I live an hour's drive west and can easily go there to ponder what I know so little about—the true nature of my family's migration versus what is preserved in family oral tradition. The migration story ends at Sunnyside Mesa, but I will have more to say about the place.

My family's migration story is notable for its omissions. It lacks psychological, emotional, and spiritual depth. And with one exception, the story omits a significant group of people, the Ute Indians. When Elija and his eight sons arrived in Colorado, they settled on land still recognized as the traditional territory and the continuing domain of the Ute. A treaty in 1868 created a much smaller Ute reservation west of the Continental Divide. Soon afterward, my great-grandfather established a new ranch on former Ute land. In 1874, the Brunot Agreement opened to prospectors a strip of Ute-held mountaintops in the San Juans, and the town of Ouray was founded a year later. In 1881, the Ute were virtually banished to Utah, with the exception of a few who were allowed to remain on a narrow strip along the New Mexico border—a strip that included Sunnyside Mesa. The much-diminished Ute reservation came within a few miles of Durango, and Durangoans launched a campaign to open even that marginal land to white settlement. In 1899, the "Ute Strip" was opened by presidential proclamation. Most of the new farms quickly failed, victims of shallow soil and little rain. A few years later my grandfather moved his family onto one of those abandoned farms.

There is one brief mention of Ute Indians in my family's history, and it is revealing. In "Oak Dell," her written account of life at the ranch, my great-grandmother Ruth Eggleston mentions a task assigned to my grandmother, Myra. The family kept a switch by the door, and little Myra used it to keep begging Ute Indians from entering the house. They were fed outside the house and never allowed to enter it. There is no mention in "Oak Dell" of the series of treaties and agreements that quickly reduced once-vast Ute hunting and gathering areas to the point that the Ute were forced to choose between begging and starvation. Neither is there any mention that the 40-mile-long spread grazed by Oak Dell cattle was virtually the heartland of the traditional domain so recently taken.

*I've been thinking lately about the relationship of archaeological research to longer-established oral histories of 2,000 years of Pueblo Indian civilization. Puebloan oral history preserves accounts of important past events at the same time it communicates the religious symbolism, high moral standards, and deeply held values of Puebloan cultures. Archaeology, in contrast, seeks to free itself of values and view the archaeological record with scientific objectivity.*

*Puebloan oral history and archaeological research in the San Juan River Basin sometimes complement each another, but not always. Puebloan oral historians, like the original tellers of the Old Testament, are not bound by units of time measured in exact years, decades, or centuries. For archaeologists, material changes measured that way are virtually the foundation of knowledge.*

*Oral histories, too, place little emphasis on the specific locations of important events. It would be no more practical to wander around the Four Corners country looking for the Place of Emergence than it would be to use the Old Testament to locate the Garden of Eden.... Archaeological research, on the other hand, is virtually defined by maps aligned to the cardinal directions and covered with lines and dots.*

*Where Puebloan oral history and archaeological research can complement each other, leading to a greater understanding of the whole, is in perceiving the human context of human places. Our perceptions of a place like Jerusalem are now so rooted in both the Old Testament and modern archaeological research that we cannot separate the two in our minds. Jerusalem's past thus becomes symbolic and real, its significance for all humanity, not just Judeo-Christian cultures, understood. Puebloan oral history and archaeology could merge in the same way, creating a greater, more human understanding of places like Cliff Palace. Puebloan oral history and scientific archaeological research do not have to agree in order to achieve that result. The two traditions already know where they disagree; no time need be wasted in arguing irreconcilable differences.*

—Ian Thompson
"Four Corners Almanac"[2]

**The stagecoach provided public transportation for the early communities of Southwest Colorado. This stage is at a stop in Dolores, Colorado.** Photo courtesy of Colorado Historical Society (20100727).

In 1962, while I was a student at the University of Colorado, my mother invited me to accompany her on an odyssey of sorts. She was becoming the unofficial historian of her branch of the Eggleston family, and wanted to retrace the family migration route from the time of Elija's arrival in 1860 to her parents' move to Sunnyside Mesa in 1911. We spent several days completing the journey. I gained visual impressions of familiar places I'd heard about in a story told to me countless times from the beginning of my memory. I gained little more. Somehow, according to our migration story, life in these places had always been good. No explanation existed for why the family stayed in one place for a while and then moved on. I ended that journey with a mental image of those places as always bathed in soft and shining Indian-summer light.

A few years later, probably as a result of too many years as a student in Boulder during the sixties, I became somewhat obsessed with my family's "psychohistory." Where was the dark side in my family's migration story—the unrequited loves, the infidelities, the unloved children, the avarice, the failures? I questioned my mother along these lines. She could invoke several different types of silence. My questions brought out her "pressed lips and tea water" silence—that is, she looked out across the sunlit Victorian rooftops of Durango, rose from her chair, and went into the kitchen to boil water for tea. I knew it was futile to pursue my questions further. I recruited two cousins to question their parents, two of whom were my mother's siblings, about the family's history along the same lines. They called back to report similar responses.

I wasn't quite ready to give up. After my mother died, I visited two elderly farm women on Sunnyside Mesa who had known my grandparents. From the time of its settlement on the opening of the Ute Strip, Sunnyside Mesa was the name of a mesa and a rural community centered on its own Grange hall, country schoolhouse, and cemetery. On hearing my questions, the Sunnyside Mesa matriarchs were incredulous at my presumptuousness and lack of good taste. Though their reasons were different, the responses I got from my family and members of the Sunnyside Mesa community when I pressed for details of my own ancestral past were remarkably similar to those of Pueblo Indian community leaders.

One of the women, several years older than my mother and her close friend throughout her life, was a person who had inspired my curiosity even as a young child. She lived

**A young Sunnyside Mesa homesteader at his morning chores, ca. 1915.** Photo courtesy of La Plata County Historical Society.

alone in an isolated farmhouse. I asked my mother why she lived alone. My mother pressed her lips together and went into the kitchen. Being young, I persisted. I gradually concluded that my mother knew some terrible secret about the woman. It was not until I was in my thirties that I learned the secret. The woman was divorced! Among the ladies of Sunnyside Mesa, the word "divorce" was never spoken.

It didn't take me long to conclude that I wasn't going to learn much about my ancestors' psychohistory from their peers on Sunnyside Mesa. I broadened my questions to include their impressions of early times in the community in general. My grandmother's and mother's friends relaxed. There were hayrides, sleigh rides, house raisings, barn raisings, piano recitals, school plays, Grange dances, and ditch cleanings. There were the rallyings to help a neighbor who'd broken a leg at planting time, or fallen ill at harvest time. What they wanted to talk about, and wanted me to remember, was community in the most positive sense of the word. I finally abandoned my attempts to know more about my family's secrets because I realized that, if they existed, they were also the community's secrets.

What are the differences between my family's migration story and those of groups or clans within modern Puebloan communities? I have available to me only written ethnographic versions of Pueblo migration stories, but they are filled with examples of human frailty, imperfection, error, and failure. They possess great psychological, emotional, and spiritual depth. These are absent from my family's migration story.

I've become increasingly convinced that the Sunnyside Mesa community was more important to my mother and her friends than was the story of how they got there. Sunnyside Mesa, like many rural American farming communities, was and is a bastion of traditional Protestant values. Deviation from the norms dictated by those values was and is punished by the community. Thus, one does not reveal one's deviations from traditional Protestant ethics. And when speaking to outsiders, if you have nothing good to say, then

**A Sunnyside Mesa homestead, ca. 1915.** Photo courtesy of La Plata County Historical Society.

you say nothing at all—bad news reflects poorly on the community as a whole. One result of this is that Sunnyside Mesa oral histories tend to sound like Christmas letters sent by one generation to the next. Only the *good* news gets in.

For differing reasons, secrecy is as important to the preservation of the Sunnyside Mesa community, and countless others like it, as it is to the preservation of modern Puebloan communities.

I recently reread a history of Durango and surrounding communities by Fort Lewis College history professor Duane Smith. He wrote of the land rush caused by the opening of the Ute Strip in 1899, including Sunnyside Mesa:

> Some violence came in the aftermath—one of the claimants for land that James Frazier staked shot him. He survived, however, to homestead his parcel.... Undesirables moved in along with the rest, and it took awhile to weed them out.... For those who stayed, life on the homestead was harsh indeed. Frazier wrote, "Many a time we all wished we had never...left sunny Kansas." Another old-timer who grew up on a Sunnyside homestead would not talk to the author about it seventy years later, so grim were his memories. For years irrigation was nonexistent, grubbing the land backbreaking, rainfall unpredictable, isolation stupefying, transportation poor, and the comforts of life few and far between. Days in a tar paper shack created dismal memories.[3]

The old-timer Smith mentioned was the uncontested patriarch of Sunnyside Mesa. Perhaps unwittingly, he said more about the history of Sunnyside Mesa and, by extension, of my family than anyone I've interrogated over the years.

I now live outside the geographical boundaries of the Sunnyside community but continue to consider myself a third-generation member of it. I and most of my generation are in our mid-fifties. Few of us lead well-ordered lives when measured against Sunnyside standards, and I've often thought we would be more self-forgiving if our ancestors had passed down more open and frank accounts of their lives.

A few years ago a friend of mine who lived on the East Coast was experiencing the early symptoms of AIDS. He told me he was contemplating suicide. I spent many hours listening to his tortured self-condemnation. His greatest fear was that, after his death, the truth about his life and illness would get back to his family and friends in the Midwest. I pleaded with him to discuss his illness with his immediate family. I was sure they would be both loving and forgiving. He came, I think, to see me as somewhat untrustworthy.

My friend eventually died, and I wrote the obituary. It described his many major achievements in life. Neither the obituary nor the eulogy I later gave at his funeral, before his family and friends, made any mention of his illness or the cause of death. Now, when I'm asked by those who knew him for details of my friend's life and death, I excuse myself, go into the kitchen, and boil water for tea.[4]

# Afterword

✳

The two of us walked slowly among aspen trees. It was springtime, and the buds on the willows were about ready to burst, the grass had yet to turn green, and the lilies in the pond stretched out before us had a long time to go before their tropical-like blossoms would reflect off the murky water.

He put his hand on my shoulder and motioned me to stop. Kneeling, his large hands gently pulled away the dry, brown grass to reveal a cluster of eggs, freckled with brown spots.

After he was sure that I had seen them, he pushed the grass back over the nest, careful not to touch the eggs. Finally, he softly spoke: "Snowy plover."

Two and one-half decades later, these words still resonate through my mind. This may or may not be my first memory of Ian Thompson, but it's certainly one of the most lasting. I must have been four years old, meaning Ian, my father, was a few years older than I am now.

It was a simple act, no more than a father showing his son something that the two of them stumbled across while walking around a pond one morning. But it is that very simplicity—I realize now, three years after my father's death—that makes the moment significant; that makes it a lasting symbol of who he was and how he had such an impact on the communities in which he was involved.

He was not one to lecture or to force knowledge into his sons' heads. He did not, on that mountain morning many springs ago, describe migratory or mating habits or tell me the Latin name of the snowy plover. Instead, he let the grass speak, let the silence sing, and let the world be the lecturer.

As is the case in any father-and-son relationship, ours did not remain this simple. And it was about the time that I was developing my own consciousness of the world around me that something caught my father's attention and held on to it. It was a humble little school housed in a few modest buildings in a hardly noticeable draw named Crow Canyon.

Long before that, my father had been a journalist. Or at least he held that position. I doubt that he was too successful in the role of detached, objective observer—the trait

allegedly required of a good journalist. Instead, he found himself getting involved in the issues he was supposed to be covering and, at various times in his life, he pursued social, political, environmental, and economic issues as they related to the land to which he was inextricably connected.

While he never dropped any of these issues entirely, it was the Crow Canyon Archaeological Center, and archaeology in its different forms, to which he devoted most of his writing, his entire professional life, and even much of his personal life. His interest in Crow Canyon quickly went far beyond a journalistic one; before long he became Crow Canyon's most outspoken advocate and an important contributor to the great body of archaeological research, in spite of his lack of formal education in the field.

Whether out of arrogance, teenage rebellion, or legitimate concerns, I was never able to completely understand his devotion to archaeology. I was quick to condemn it as utterly materialistic; concentrating not on the human soul, heart, or mind, but solely on the objects left behind. To me it was an esoteric pursuit, conducted by technicians who were quick to put various artifacts into seemingly arbitrary categories, but who failed to think about the motives, dreams, and desires of the craftsman or artist who created them.

I wondered how one could devote so much time and energy to sifting through the artifacts of ancient Puebloans when the very descendants of those people were fighting for their own cultural survival only a few hours' drive south. Where, I wondered, is the humanity in archaeology? For a long time it seemed to me that my father should be spending his resources on things which were easier for the contemporary world to relate to and on which he could exert some influence.

I look back on that time and my views with embarrassment, and wonder now how I could have been so blind to what was always right in front of me.

The two of us spent a great deal of our time together walking around the rubble of ancient pueblos. More often than not, we searched for what he called "architecture with unknown function"—manmade berms, rows of aligned stones, and other features for which there was no acceptable explanation. Each discovery was inevitably followed by a conversation between the two of us, each offering a theory of the feature's purpose and the motive behind its construction.

I would almost habitually offer an astronomical explanation based on my recent studies of Ptolemy in college, or even explain the features as merely decorative in much the same way that an arrangement of stones in a modern garden might be. My father would actually listen to my theories without judgment and would offer his own and relate those of Rina Swentzell or Tessie Naranjo.

To me, these little trips were fascinating, but our speculation seemed at the time to be little more than an intellectual exercise. It was not until fairly recently, during a third or fourth reading of this book's manuscript, that I realized that what we were doing during those jaunts through the piñon, juniper, sage, and rubble. It was, albeit in an undisciplined form, archaeology. On each visit to a site, my father drew from and added to a vast bank of knowledge gleaned from reading countless texts, dozens of conversations with archaeologists and Native Americans, and literally hundreds of similar walks where he pored over rubble and room blocks and examined the surrounding horizon, marking the relative locations of geographical and astronomical features.

His insatiable quest for a deeper understanding of these sites and the people who once inhabited them was not limited to purely conventional archaeological research. He was not afraid to borrow from his knowledge of the more recent history of the area, as he did in the first chapter of this book comparing the movement of Puebloan communities to that of Ackmen. Nor did he fear borrowing from his own experiences, as he did in the last chapter.

I read the first chapters of this book—what would turn

**The old Elco Post Office, just south of Sunnyside Mesa, ca. 1911.**
Photo courtesy of La Plata County Historical Society.

**Sandy Thompson (right) with Vernon Lujan (Taos Pueblo), in 1994. Sandy worked to integrate archaeological research with Native American perspectives and traditional knowledge. His work in this vein has become an important part of Crow Canyon's mission.** © Crow Canyon Archaeological Center, 1994.

out to be the only chapters—in the early spring of 1998. I could not help but feel then that the words were speaking directly to me, a feeling that has grown stronger with each successive reading. And, with those readings, many of the questions and doubts I had about my father's apparent obsession with archaeology and with Crow Canyon were answered. These pages, for me, connected the humanity with the archaeology.

Sadly, I could never communicate that long-delayed revelation with my father, who died only weeks after my first reading of the book. And, unfortunately, he would never write again—never finish this, his final work. I believe it is, even with its abrupt and unfinished ending, his finest.

When I was asked to write this afterword to try to explain how important archaeology was to my father, and to try to sum up what the rest of the book might have looked like, I was baffled and even ashamed. My earlier disdain of archaeology certainly disqualified me for such a task; my brother Geoffrey, who is himself an archaeologist, would be much more competent. Regardless, I chose to accept the job and I have struggled with it as much as I have with any piece of writing.

This book was to be the expression of the knowledge my father amassed over his lifetime of walking and watching this country, its rhythms, and its peoples. It was to be about Crow Canyon, the research done there, and, maybe just as important, the diverse group of people who have conducted that research. We see the beginning of this work in the pages that were completed and, by taking us through the actual archaeological process itself, he shows us that these scientists are by no means the cold-hearted technicians I had once accused them of being.

Missing is the chapter on Native American viewpoints and the link that my father was devoted to fostering between archaeology and the oral histories of the modern Pueblos. Such a link, he hoped, would not only add to the archaeological record, but it could also enrich the Puebloans' view of their own story.

Also missing is the chapter explaining how Crow Canyon's research was anything but esoteric, opening itself up to thousands of students each year who participated in, learned from, and even enhanced the archaeologists' work. Education, to Crow Canyon and to my father, is just as important as research. And there almost certainly would have been a chapter devoted to my father's own thoughts on archaeology.

One of the original possibilities for the posthumous completion of this work was to try to recreate each of those chapters as my father would have written them. We abandoned that idea quickly, realizing how disjointed such an attempt, if we could do it, would read. It would be just as foolhardy for me to attempt to go into the details here of what the book might have contained.

But a primary theme is already apparent in the finished chapters and runs through almost all of my father's writing: the inclusive and sometimes evasive theme of community. His exploration of community, which includes people, place, and time, was both a personal and universal one. It was part of a struggle to understand his place in this harsh and beautiful landscape, along with a quest to add to the greater Four Corners community's understanding of itself.

Archaeology ultimately became his primary mode of exploration, something he used to understand the interaction between the people and the landscape. Given the importance he placed on the past, on the stories that led each culture and community to its present place, archaeology was an obvious choice.

This book was intended to be the story of the community of Crow Canyon, of Ackmen, of Duckfoot, of Sand Canyon, and of pueblos present and past. It was neither a detached, journalistic venture, nor an academic compilation of research. Rather, it was a selfless gift: the ultimate product of a man's quest for a greater understanding of himself, his community, the landscape that shaped both, and of the past that shaped them all.

It was to be a simple gesture, universally understood, like a father pulling aside a clump of dried grass, revealing one of nature's wonders to his son.

✳

He walked quickly through the piñon and juniper, a bounce in his step. I matched his pace about 10 feet away. It was a hot, early summer afternoon, and this was the third site we visited that day. The trees opened up to a sagebrush-covered mound scattered with rubble and potsherds. We were not interested in the mound which was once a cluster of room blocks, plazas, and kivas.

The routine was familiar, and as my father walked one way, I went the other, circling the mound but staying at a distance from it, my eyes scanning the ground. When I saw the first, large, lichen-covered stone, I started to get excited. But it was not until I found the fourth such stone, lined up perfectly with the first three, that I knew I had found what we were looking for.

I continued piecing the row of stones together until he walked up, his circle complete. "What did you find, Jon?"

"Look," I replied, trying to keep the excitement out of my voice. I showed him the rest of the line, silently. Then I pulled the compass out of the backpack and placed it on one of the rocks. The line, far from the pueblo and with no apparent purpose, ran directly east and west.

We stood silently, listening to the wind whisper in the trees and a cicada chirping in the distance. The Sleeping Ute loomed a dark blue behind us. I was 25 years old and he was 55. For a moment, the magic of that morning so long ago returned.

—**Jonathan Thompson**
Silverton, Colorado
2001

**Castle Rock Pueblo in McElmo Canyon.** Photo courtesy of Colorado Historical Society (10028079).

# Notes

✳

## Chapter one

[1] Paul S. Martin, "The 1929 Archaeological Expedition of the State Historical Society of Colorado in Cooperation with the Smithsonian Institution," *Colorado Magazine* (January 1930). Reprinted courtesy of the Colorado Historical Society.

## Chapter two

[1] John Wesley Powell, *Canyons of the Colorado* (Flood and Vincent: 1895).

[2] J. S. Newberry, "Report of the Exploring Expedition from Santa Fe, New Mexico, to the Junction of the Grand and Green Rivers of the Great Colorado of the West, in 1859" (Washington: Government Printing Office, 1876).

[3] Ian Thompson, "Four Corners Almanac," *The Durango Herald* (October 11, 1992).

## Chapter three

[1] Ian Thompson, "Four Corners Almanac," *The Durango Herald* (April 3, 1994).

[2] Ian Thompson, "Four Corners Almanac," *The Durango Herald* (March 6, 1994).

[3] Crow Canyon's current policy is to emphasize preservation by excavating only a small percentage of any given site. After a fashion, Duckfoot also represents a sample—in this case because it is only one of several hamlets in a dispersed community.

[4] Ian Thompson, "Four Corners Almanac," *The Durango Herald* (February 10, 1985).

[5] Since 1987, the Crow Canyon Archaeological Center, in consultation with its Native American advisory group, has adopted a policy of avoiding, if possible, the excavation of burials and leaving human remains undisturbed when they are discovered during excavation.

## Chapter four

[1] Alfred Castner King, "Dolores," in *The Passing of the Storm and Other Poems* (Fleming H. Revell Co., 1907).

[2] Research by other Crow Canyon archaeologists, notably Michael Adler, professor of anthropology at Southern Methodist University, and Mark Varien, forged more comprehensive definitions of ancient communities in the early 1990s.

[3] Ian Thompson, "Four Corners Almanac," *The Durango Herald* (September 17, 1995).

[4] Archaeologists acknowledge that these somewhat arbitrary boundaries and regions are the creations of early twentieth-century scholars who were beginning to recognize differences among ancient Puebloan cultures in the Southwest.

[5] Ian Thompson, "Four Corners Almanac," *The Durango Herald* (August 4, 1991).

[6] Ian Thompson, "Four Corners Almanac," *The Durango Herald* (March 13, 1994).

## Chapter five

[1] Ian Thompson, "Four Corners Almanac," *The Durango Herald* (August 10, 1986).

[2] Ian Thompson, "Four Corners Almanac," *The Durango Herald* (August 13, 1995).

[3] This chapter is a slightly revised version of an article by Ian Thompson that was originally published in *Archaeology* (Volume 48, Number 5), titled "The Search for Settlements on the Great Sage Plain." Copyright by The Archaeological Institute of America, 1995. Reprinted with permission of the publisher.

## Chapter six

[1] Ian Thompson, "Four Corners Almanac," *The Durango Herald* (June 6, 1993).

[2] Ian Thompson, "Four Corners Almanac," *The Durango Herald* (June 27, 1993).

[3] This chapter is a revised version of a chapter that was originally published in the book *Anasazi Architecture and American Design*, edited by Baker H. Morrow and V.B. Price (University of New Mexico Press, 1997). Ian Thompson was the senior author of the original manuscript; Mark Varien, Susan Kenzle, and Rina Swentzell were coauthors. Reprinted with permission of the publisher.

## Chapter seven

[1] Ian Thompson, "Four Corners Almanac," *The Durango Herald* (September 24, 1995).

[2] Ian Thompson, "Four Corners Almanac," *The Durango Herald* (August 2, 1992).

[3] Duane A. Smith, *Rocky Mountain Boom Town: A History of Durango* (University Press of Colorado, 1992). Reprinted with permission of the author.

[4] Chapter 7 was originally a paper presented under the title *"Secrecy in Oral Tradition"* at the 1994 Chacmool Conference at the University of Calgary and is published here with permission of Ian Thompson's sons, Geoffrey and Jonathan Thompson.

# EarthTales Press *"Listen to the Earth and the tales it has to tell..."*

Since 1981, Westcliffe Publishers has produced quality guidebooks, coffee-table books, and calendars—works that celebrate nature's wonders through full-color scenic photography. Westcliffe's EarthTales Press imprint views the natural world through a different lens: the compelling words of acclaimed wilderness writers. EarthTales Press explores the human relationship with the environment and encourages readers to develop both physical and spiritual connections with our treasured wildlands.

## Other EarthTales Press titles include:

### Land of Grass and Sky: A Naturalist's Prairie Journey
#### By Mary Taylor Young

Part nature lore, part history, part meditation, the author's account of her lifelong odyssey through the austere yet beautiful shortgrass prairie weaves an intricate landscape of wildlife, plants, and people. To look beyond the open space, to truly know a prairie and its secrets, the author looks inward to find that despite the changing face of the plains, the prairie's lesson remains the same: As we learn to appreciate this subtle, hard-to-love land, we come to value ourselves. ISBN 1-56579-431-1

### Living on the Spine: A Woman's Life in the Sangre de Cristo Mountains
#### By Christina Nealson

Through journal-style passages that follow the movement of the seasons, Christina Nealson chronicles her courageous five-year journey into solitude at the foot of Colorado's Sangre de Cristo range. Her stirring descriptions of the landscape paint a clear picture of life in the high desert, and her captivating story blends the simplicity of her lifestyle with the intricacy of the human spirit. By living gently, honestly, and passionately, Nealson cuts life to the core to discover the truths of a woman's soul. ISBN 1-56579-471-0

### PrueHeart the Wanderer: From Western Wilderness to Concrete Canyons
#### By Lynna Howard

Idaho-based Lynna Howard—alias PrueHeart the Wanderer—discovers wildness in the heart of New York City just as easily as she does in the fringes of her home state. PrueHeart's urban adventures juxtapose her witty, insightful travel diary entries and poetry written on wilderness treks throughout the American West. The interplay she creates between urban and backcountry experiences reveals much about the connection of the two "wilds" and redefines exploration as anything that stretches the spirit and inspires the soul. ISBN 1-56579-432-X

### Stone Desert: A Naturalist's Exploration of Canyonlands National Park
#### By Craig Childs

For the length of a winter, author and National Public Radio commentator Craig Childs traveled the mysterious and desolate Canyonlands National Park in Utah—a region full of shadows and surreal sandstone shapes. Within this landscape, geology becomes a language of poetry. Botany turns to the taste of a leaf on the tongue. The author followed paths of rivers, chasms, and sensual backs of stone to emerge the following spring with a journal in his hands. Its drawings and text became this book, a search for order and understanding in an enigmatic desert. ISBN 1-56579-473-7

### Under the Arctic Sun: Gwich'in, Caribou, and the Arctic National Wildlife Refuge
#### By Ken Madsen

Award-winning author and conservationist Ken Madsen has hiked, paddled, photographed, and championed some of North America's most remote wilderness. Since 1998, he has coordinated the Caribou Commons Project, an international effort to preserve the coastal plain of northeastern Alaska's Arctic National Wildlife Refuge from industrial oil and gas development. An adventure story, naturalist's journal, personal account, and call to action, Madsen's narrative is witty and thoroughly engaging. It is an appeal to human rights, to the dignity of ancient species, and to careful stewardship of what is left on Earth of true wilderness. ISBN 1-56579-466-4